Making a Successful Jewish Interfaith Marriage

Making a Successful Jewish Interfaith Marriage

The Jewish Outreach Institute
Guide to Opportunities,
Challenges and Resources

Rabbi Kerry M. Olitzky
with Joan Peterson Littman

Preface by Terrence A. Elkes, President,
Jewish Outreach Institute

JEWISH LIGHTS Publishing
Woodstock, Vermont

Making a Successful Jewish Interfaith Marriage:
The Jewish Outreach Institute Guide to Opportunities, Challenges and Resources

© 2003 by Kerry M. Olitzky

Grateful acknowledgment is given for permission to use material from *Embracing the Covenant: Converts to Judaism Talk About Why and How,* by Allan L. Berkowitz and Patti Moskovitz, copyright © 1996, used by permission of Jewish Lights Publishing.

Library of Congress Cataloging-in-Publication Data
Olitzky, Kerry M.
Making a successful Jewish interfaith marriage : the Jewish Outreach Institute guide to opportunities, challenges, and resources / Kerry M. Olitzky with Joan Peterson Littman ; preface by Terrence A. Elkes.
       p.   cm.
Includes bibliographical references.
ISBN 1-58023-170-5 (pbk.)
1. Interfaith marriage. 2. Marriage—Religious aspects—Judaism. 3. Interfaith families. 4. Jewish families—Religious life. I. Littman, Joan Peterson. II. Title.
HQ1031 .O45 2003
306.84'3—dc21

                                                              2002015857

10 9 8 7 6 5 4 3 2 1

Manufactured in the United States of America

Published by Jewish Lights Publishing
A Division of LongHill Partners, Inc.
Sunset Farm Offices, Route 4, P.O. Box 237
Woodstock, VT 05091
Tel: (802) 457-4000   Fax: (802) 457-4004
www.jewishlights.com

For our children,
Avi and Jesse Olitzky,
Sarah and Anne Littman,
and for all children.

CONTENTS

Contents

PREFACE

This is a book *about* interfaith relationships *for* interfaith couples. It is also for all those members of your family who love you, even if they have not fully accepted the decision you have made—or even understand that decision. Their love for you may be obscured by the heated discussions and arguments that have recently emerged, much to your surprise and consternation, but it is there just the same. Our goal is to help you bring this love back to the fore through understanding and open dialogue. We recognize that this is not an easy task. It is made easier, however, by the fact that it, like the relationship you are developing with your partner, is built on a primary foundation of love.

Your love for each other may lead you to marriage, if it hasn't already done so. The Jewish community will call it an intermarriage and may even—consciously or unconsciously—try to punish you by pushing you to the side, making you feel unwelcome. This is the way communities tend to deal with members who follow controversial paths in life. This route is becoming more common. The rate of interfaith marriage in the Jewish community is over 50 percent nationwide, and it is on the rise. Interfaith marriages among other communities are also taking place in greater numbers. This is leading us to an increasingly multicultural society, where it is all the more important to address interfaith issues. Leaders of the Jewish community are concerned, as they have always been. They are worried—as they should be—about the impact of intermarriage on the Jewish future. So they spend a lot of time talking about numbers, and developing strategies to respond to the realities these numbers represent.

We believe that statistics should be reserved for other discussions. We are interested primarily in people and in how their decisions to marry out of their faith affects their relationship and their spirituality. So while this book may make mention of some statistics and insights we have gained from studying the American Jewish population, this book is not about numbers. Rather, it is about people: you and the one you love, as well as the many people, family, and friends who want to find a way to keep you in their hearts and in their lives—even if, at this point, they have not permitted themselves the freedom to do so.

Many in the Jewish community see interfaith marriage as a crisis, contributing to the demographic changes that threaten the faith's very survival. We see intermarriage as an *opportunity*—an opportunity to stem the downward spiral of population decline and instead add people to its ranks. We believe that interfaith marriage encourages both partners to confront their feelings about religion in a profound way that often deepens their spiritual commitment. We see interfaith marriage as a relationship between two people, one who happens to be Jewish and one who happens not to be, rather than as numbers in a zero-sum game.

Intermarriage is not a failure of our community or its institutions. Rather, it is a by-product of America's open society. It presents a challenge for the community to reach out and embrace those who have found their way into our midst as a result of a loving relationship. It calls on us to create institutions of meaning for all those with a spiritual thirst and hunger, regardless of the path that brought the individual to the Jewish community.

Each of you who reads this book is participating in the process of shaping the future of the Jewish community. We join you on your journey. We support each step that you take and each decision that you make, and we are here to help you along the way.

Terrence A. Elkes
President, Jewish Outreach Institute

ACKNOWLEDGMENTS

Who knew when Avi brought Sarah home that *his* father (Kerry) and *her* mother (Joan) would eventually write a book together about the challenges and successes of interfaith marriage? Who knew that Kerry—after leading a congregation in West Hartford, Connecticut, and teaching at Hebrew Union College–Jewish Institute of Religion, the rabbinical seminary of the Reform movement, then moving on to become vice president of the Wexner Heritage Foundation, the premier adult Jewish learning program in North America—would bring these experiences together to become the executive director of the Jewish Outreach Institute, the only national organization devoted to reaching unaffiliated Jews with an emphasis on providing services to the intermarried and their children? Who knew that Joan, brought up as a practicing Lutheran, would fall in love with Larry Littman, marry him, and raise a Jewish family? Who knew that Joan would become the person in a small synagogue in Troy, Michigan, who works alongside its rabbi to support and nurture interfaith couples and their families? Such is the stuff of life and the reality of our faith in the Source of all life.

One thing we both know for sure is that none of this is coincidence. These journeys brought us together to prepare this volume under the auspices of the Jewish Outreach Institute for Jewish Lights Publishing. While we are grateful for the opportunity to do this together, there are many people to be thanked. In particular, we mention Jewish Lights publisher Stuart M. Matlins and his wife, Antoinette, friends whose inclusive vision for Jewish publishing and the community mirrors our own. They continually offer the opportunity to stand on their shoulders and climb higher. As filled with words as this book is, there are no words that can express what we feel about these two wonderful people. We are particularly appreciative of the time Stuart took to edit this volume, since the development of an inclusive Jewish community is a subject dear to his heart. We also want to thank the wonderful members of the staff at Jewish Lights Publishing, particularly Jon Sweeney and Emily Wichland, who have guided and supported this effort from conception through production and distribution, recognizing the importance of its mission. We also thank Elisheva Urbas, who helped us frame the book from its beginning, and Judith D. Schwartz, who served as our editor.

We also express our appreciation to Jenny Jacobi and Laura Samberg for reviewing some of the material contained in these pages, as well as Rabbi Nancy Weiner for her help.

We thank the board members and professional colleagues at the Jewish Outreach Institute who opened up the door for so many, particularly Terry Elkes, president; Paul Golin, director of communications, who read this book in manuscript form and made countless suggestions for its improvement; Alex Unger, assistant executive director, who shares the passion for our work; and Joseph Zargari, program assistant, for help in preparing the resources that appear at the end of the book. In addition, we acknowledge Gail Quets, director of research; Hannah Greenstein, program officer; Ivana Bradanovic, office manager; and Denyse Gregoire, database manager and conference coordinator. None of the work at the Jewish Outreach Institute would be possible without them.

We thank our families and our children for providing us the love and support out of which this book was made.

Above all, we offer our gratitude to the Source of all life, who sought to merge our paths in life through our children and through our life's work so that we could take this enlightening journey together.

Rabbi Kerry ("Shia") Olitzky
Joan Peterson Littman

A Special Note
for Parents

While this book was written primarily for intermarried couples and for those contemplating intermarriage, this book is also for you, their parents. We raise our children to make independent decisions, yet may be taken aback when they demonstrate considerable skill in doing exactly as they were taught. Perhaps we expect our children to make the same decisions that we would make in similar circumstances. In the choice of a life partner, it is important for us to remember that the social world of our children is dramatically different from the one we traveled in at their age. They are likely to be exposed to far more people from a broad range of backgrounds than we ever were.

Often the decision to marry someone from a different faith distances children from their parents and other members of their families, as well as from their religious communities. Being aware of this risk may motivate you to bridge the potential gap. In your consternation and confusion as parents, you will no doubt experience a vast spectrum of emotions such as anger, embarrassment, abandonment, betrayal, or even depression. You may feel guilty, perhaps wondering whether leading a more religious life would have altered your child's choices. You may feel that you've failed. Your self-esteem may take a beating. And you will undoubtedly wonder how you will be judged by your friends and religious community. Perhaps you are particularly concerned about the opinion of a family patriarch or matriarch whose approval you cherish.

While most parents who read this book will not take such drastic actions as saying *kaddish* for or disinheriting their child, some distancing may take place nonetheless, even if such distancing is subtle. When you reject the person whom your son or daughter brings home to marry, you unintentionally may reject him or her as an "outsider." This "outsider" is often the butt of anti-Gentile or anti-Jewish sentiments. Stereotypic references, jokes, and derisive terms for other people can promote the disengagement of a child from his family. This may put your child on the defensive. It may even drive him or her to choose one set of parents over the other.

When an intermarriage raises the voltage to an already volatile parent/child relationship, professional therapeutic intervention may be warranted. But by pointing out the tools you likely already have to work things out, this book may help. And so will lots of love.

A SPECIAL NOTE FOR JEWISH COMMUNITY LEADERS

Out of three million Jewish households, there are one million inter-married households in the United States. This is the reality of con-temporary Jewish life. Some community leaders have chosen to reject those who have intermarried and, psychologically or institu-tionally, punish them for doing so. We have chosen instead to embrace them, because we believe that love is a stronger force than is hate. And we do not see a million people who have married out; instead, we see the potential of a million married people who have chosen to marry into the Jewish community. By reaching out to interfaith families and by helping them make Jewish choices for themselves and their families, we have the opportunity to rebuild the North American Jewish community, where numbers are dwin-dling naturally because of an aging society and below-zero popula-tion growth.

We encourage you to welcome these families and their chil-dren, as we have chosen to do. As Rabbi Rachel Cowan, an advo-cate for the intermarried, says, this will take "openness, risk, and initiative." Open your homes, schools, and synagogues to them. Above all else, open your hearts.

A SPECIAL NOTE
FOR RABBIS

For many years I listened to teachers and colleagues debate the future of the Jewish community, condemning interfaith marriage as the root cause of the slow erosion of Jewish continuity. They blamed the growing irrelevance of synagogues on the phenomenon of intermarriage, distancing themselves from any responsibility. For some unknown reason, it was easier for them to push away than to embrace. This "ain't it awful" approach has to stop. It may be slowing as intermarriage gains more acceptance by families who realize that religion, philosophy, theology, and practice are not nearly as sweet as the hug of a grandchild. And it may be slowing as religious leaders try to renew their institutions and build new ones, recognizing that the ones that now cover the landscape of the American Jewish community are failing to offer the spiritual sustenance that so many seek. It is finally time for those of us at the center of the Jewish community to speak out and tell the truth, while guiding those who seek direction for their daily lives. That is why I decided to write this book.

I have spent most of my rabbinate helping to build institutions that nurture and support Jewish identity and encouraging participation in them: day schools, Jewish summer camps, synagogue youth programs, extended trips to Israel. I continue to believe in them as primary institutional sources of Jewish continuity. But even if these formative Jewish institutions were to work flawlessly and effectively, the phenomenon of interfaith marriage would not cease. It is an inevitable part of modern life. And even if there were to be no more interfaith marriages from this day forward, there would still remain one million interfaith households in the United States—fully one third of all the Jewish family homes in this country. Interfaith marriages are not a result of our failure in North America. Rather, they are the product of our successes.

Where we have failed is in our inability to see interfaith marriage as an opportunity rather than a problem. The United States has figured out a way to absorb thousands of new immigrants from various countries each year, particularly those from the former Soviet Union, but we have not figured out a way to absorb the thousands of non-Jews who marry into Jewish families each year—the new immigrants in our community. Instead, we often ostracize those individuals and condemn their families to live on the outside. We shun strangers and forbid them access to our communal institutions, forcing them to the periphery and then wondering why they do not enter of their own accord, claiming that they were lost in the first place. By *our* actions, we punish them for *their* actions. Even our vocabulary and our descriptions of such family situations characterize them as "other."

This book neither condones nor condemns intermarriage. It is not its place to do so. Like the Rabbis of the Talmud who make a legal distinction between those things that are *behatchila* (before the fact) and those that are *bedeavad* (after the fact), this book recognizes the reality of interfaith marriage after it has taken place, even as we support and encourage in-marriage. It is difficult to make a marriage work, and it is even more difficult to make an interfaith marriage work. But I do not believe that my opinion—or this fact—necessarily has an impact on the decisions made by autonomous adults to join their lives together. Rather, I accept their decisions as part of the reality of contemporary Jewish life. And I certainly support the right of each individual to make informed choices regarding their marriage, as I would in every other important area of life.

Therefore, this book is designed to help interfaith couples and their families, but it is also for *you,* their rabbi. As you work with these couples and their families, I would urge you to remember what we all have been taught: "God creates new worlds constantly—by causing marriages to take place" (*Zohar* I, 89a).

Rabbi Kerry M. Olitzky

1

THE FACTS AND WHERE
YOU FIT IN

If you have decided to marry someone from a family whose religion is different from your own, you are far from alone. Many have made that same decision before you, and many more will make it in the future. Of this, there is no debate. It is true, however, that the numbers of interfaith marriages in this generation are greater throughout North America, irrespective of religious community, than in previous generations. (While I use the term "marriage," I recognize that there are lots of different kinds of committed relationships, and I include all of them as well.)

In the past ten years, over half of the marriages involving Jews have been to partners not born Jewish. At least one third of the three million Jewish families who identify as such in the United States have a head-of-household (this includes men and women) who was not born Jewish. About one third of the families who are members of Reform congregations are interfaith families. And over 50 percent of the children born into Jewish families in the last decade have one set of grandparents who is not Jewish. There is no reason to believe that these percentages are going to become smaller in the years ahead. This is no one's "fault." It is simply a fact in contemporary American Jewish life, a result of the open and free society that we have come to know and enjoy in America. It is another milestone in the exciting path that the Jewish people have traveled throughout our history.

These are the facts, and you are now part of these statistics. And these are the feelings that come with joining this set of numbers. As Susan Weidman Schneider, the editor of *Lilith* magazine, has observed, "Interfaith marriage is a phenomenon viewed by some Jews and Christians with alarm, by some with curiosity, and by the partners themselves as a name for their situation that represents only some of the many challenges they face in living together. The partners must at some level deal with their own and each other's feelings of loss of continuity, betraying ancestors, creating complexities in the lives of children alive and yet-to-be, of competition, anger, rejection."[1]

While some people bemoan interfaith marriages for a variety of reasons, including issues of race and a feeling of personal betrayal, we must all recognize that intermarriage is a result of Jewish *success* in America, not its failure. Many of our grandparents sought refuge in this country because of its democratic ideals. They fought for equality and an end to quotas in immigration, education, the professions, and even social clubs. They fought hard to belong, to make it easier for their progeny. We in this generation are the beneficiaries of that success, but we also bear its burden and responsibility. However, the facts of history alone do not tell the story of people's lives. For example, at one time, many Jews entered into interfaith marriages as a way of escaping the Jewish community and "passing" into the larger American society. This is no longer the primary motivation for most interfaith marriages. Few of the cultural, educational, social, or professional barriers for Jews that once motivated intermarriage remain as barriers. Similarly, there was limited social interaction between Jews and others, and fewer non-Jews were willing to marry Jews. Few people elected to become associated with a minority that had so many restrictions placed on it. This, too, is no longer the case in America today.

WHAT IS AN INTERMARRIAGE, ANYWAY?

"Intermarriage" is a term that sociologists use to describe a marriage between two people, one born into a particular faith and one born into another faith. Some people like to make a technical distinction between an *intermarriage,* where a conversion has taken place, and an *interfaith* or *mixed marriage,* where there has not been a conversion. In this book we use most of these terms interchangeably, as do most people. While these terms may present an unwelcome description of your relationship—perhaps one that you might even reject—it is a term that the Jewish community has thrust upon you. Labels are a fact of life for those who intermarry.

Although new evidence suggests that the majority of American Jews no longer hold interfaith marriages in total disdain and are choosing to just accept them as part of the Jewish communal landscape, the idea of an interfaith marriage or of interfaith dating is still considered a major "problem" by the organized Jewish community—that is, by community leaders. While many scholars debate the reason for the change in attitude among the general Jewish population, it appears to me that married children are less under the direct influence of their parents than in previous generations. As people marry at later ages, they exercise more independence. There is also a latent fear that the criterion of in-faith marriage may prevent them from marrying at all. As one man in a small community in the far West told me, "I want to marry someone who is Jewish. But I don't think that will happen for me. I have not met any Jewish women, and I'm not getting any younger."

Your dating life is not necessarily determined by the faith community you were born into. Instead, you were probably drawn to your partner for a first date (and second date and beyond) by common interests and shared values. The fact that the faith community of your family of origin may be different from the community of the person you have come to love might today have about as much relevance as the fact that your ancestors might have immigrated to North America from different foreign countries. While ancestry certainly had relevance back then, such distinctions may no longer have any conscious bearing on your life, either on the decisions you make or in how the community at large regards you.

Today more people meet their future partners and spouses in the workplace, rather than in college, as was the case in the last generation. People partner and marry later in life. Couples have children later. There are higher rates of divorce, second marriages, and blended families. Thus, even the college experience (and the important work of Hillel and other organizations) has less impact on the phenomenon of interfaith marriage today than it had in previous generations. People meet and fall in love. They meet at work, at parties, and in lines at the movies. No measure of Jewish education will prevent such meetings from taking place.

MAKING THE CASE FOR OPTIMISM AND INCLUSION

I believe in the sacredness of family life and want to reduce the factors that destabilize marriages. Also, I recognize the reality of interfaith marriages and acknowledge the real challenges that interfaith couples face. I believe that once a decision to marry has been made, the Jewish community has the responsibility to do all it can to help that couple and embrace the new family that may emerge.

Some critics of intermarriage may not consider what individuals are facing and feel that they have a "higher calling" to oppose it. These critics think that wholesale condemnation will change attitudes and behaviors. That alone, they believe, will discourage the practice of Jews marrying outside their faith. The higher the intermarriage rate, the more poisonous becomes their vitriol. Studies show that this approach is ineffective in most cases. Personally I think it is wrong, morally and practically.

The statistics are real. Between 65 and 75 percent will not raise their children as Jews, reducing the likelihood that their children will learn about the Jewish tradition. That branch in a four-thousand-year-old tradition will be cut—an unfortunate trend for those of us who believe in the value of Jewish life, learning, and community. It is this trend that I am working against—not the particular makeup of couples and their families. Unwittingly, the Jewish community has contributed to this trend by simply accepting it. If the community is unwilling to do anything to change these results, the trend will continue. I believe that by opening the borders of the Jewish community, and by breaking down the barriers that have been erected to prevent interfaith families from entering, we can actually help maintain Jewish family life for a wide variety of family constellations in the process.

Jewish life has endured for four thousand years or more. It has evolved and changed and faced difficult times. The Jewish community is concerned about its continuity and survival. Make no mistake about it: I am just as concerned. I support Jewish communal institutions and want to make sure that they welcome our children, intermarried or not, because I believe that intermarriage is not the end of Jewish continuity. As a matter of fact, I think that intermarriage has the potential to add people and their talents to the community. So I see intermarried families and their children as a potential gain to the Jewish community, rather than a loss.

Placed right in the center of the Torah, in a section that has come to be called the Holiness Code because it sets the standard for Jewish behavior and is therefore among the first texts taught to young Jewish children as they embark on their Jewish education, comes the text that has framed Jewish attitudes for centuries: "The stranger that lives with you shall be to you like the native, and you shall love him [or her] as yourself; for you were strangers in the land of Egypt. I am the Lord your God" (Leviticus 19:34). There seems no question in the mind of Torah Judaism about how we are to act. And just to make sure that we understand the importance of this core value, the verse ends with "I am the Lord your God." It therefore becomes a signature text for the Jewish community. By adding this divine seal at its end, the Torah text communicates the message quite strongly, making sure the reader makes no mistake about the origin of this command. Thus, the notion of inclusion as advocated in this book has divine origins and is completely consistent with the attitude toward what the Torah calls the stranger (non-Jew) that has informed the Jewish psyche for four millennia.

Rabbis as far back as the year 500 C.E. understood the dilemma we are facing. When it was not possible to finesse a particular biblical narrative in order to accomplish their task, the Rabbis emphasized the Jewish character of the Jewish partner in the relationship. Thus, they reminded us that Queen Esther observed Judaism (and the dietary laws) in the castle while she hid her Jewish identity during her marriage to Ahashuerus, the non-Jewish king of ancient Persia. Even so, the Rabbis accepted her marriage, particularly because it was this particular interfaith marriage that eventually saved the Jews of Persia from annihilation.

While the legal system the Rabbis developed remains rather complex, they considered Jewish law from basically two perspectives. The first perspective was called *behatchila* (*a priori*, before the fact), and the second was called *bedeavad* (*a posteriori*, after the fact). And they acted accordingly. They considered events and behaviors very differently before their occurrence as opposed to after they had already taken place. As a result, I would argue that once an intermarriage has taken place, the Jewish community has a responsibility to be welcoming and inclusive to you, the intermarried or otherwise bonded. Rabbi Rachel Cowan, author of *Mixed Blessings: Overcoming the Stumbling Blocks in an Interfaith Marriage,* wrote in an article in *Moment* magazine, "A marriage that looks like a step away from the community is often a confrontation with the importance of Jewish identity. The Jewish partner, gentile spouse in hand, may be forced to ask questions about Judaism [and personal Jewish identity] that two Jews never ask [of themselves]."[2] Our goal is to help both spouses, and their families, grapple with these questions.

WHAT DO WE SUGGEST?

This guide presents a frank and honest discussion about interfaith marriages, their challenges, and their opportunities. While supportive of the decision you have made and supportive of you, it does not disguise the truth, even when it may be painful or disheartening to hear. Joining two independent lives to form the beginning of a family is not easy and may be fraught with unforeseen difficulties. For the few lucky couples, an intermarriage will be no more challenging than an in-faith marriage itself. I like to say that intermarriages are like in-faith marriages, only more so. For most people, the road ahead will not be easy. It's important to say it aloud and read it in print so that there will be no misunderstanding. Each partner's values and sense of identity will be challenged. Family ties will be strained. Difficult decisions will have to be made, such as those regarding children. And you may question the choices you have made.

Intellectually, intermarriage demands work. You can't gloss over certain ideas and traditions on the assumption that your mate "knows what you mean." You will be learning about your partner's religion, and the need to explain yours may send you back to the books. Fortunately, there are more and more friendly resources that you may not know about.

This book walks with you through your relationship, starting with navigating your relationship before marriage. While this book is relevant to anyone involved in an interfaith relationship at any stage, most readers will probably pick it up early in a relationship. So we'll start right in at your first date and help you prepare for it, and even help you prepare to meet your future in-laws. Perhaps most importantly, we'll help you evaluate and reflect on the various aspects of your relationship, including the inevitable questions about the ceremony (who's officiating and who's invited), religious choices for your children (perhaps even before you are even thinking about children), and the options for conversion (should this be a choice that you consider).

While the language and tone of this book may seem easygoing, we emphasize that the subject is far from frivolous. In chapters that follow, we'll look at relationships with parents, grandparents, and siblings (and how they are affected—and even changed— by your interfaith relationship), decisions about children, which holidays to celebrate and where to celebrate them, and life-cycle events that you will encounter in the course of family life. We'll try to help you create time and space for your own spiritual life and also take a hard look at the road ahead, honestly exploring the challenges that you will undoubtedly continue to face. Finally, we'll take into consideration those who may marry later in life and those whose family configurations may not reflect the main thrust of this volume, particularly gay and lesbian interfaith families, multiethnic/multiracial families, and couples who live together in committed relationships—and even have children—but do not marry.

While a book has to conclude at some point, the trials you face as an interfaith family will not. They may lessen over time, but you will continue to face many challenges over the course of your life together. Each new challenge may call up different aspects of Jewish religion and culture, as well as different personal needs. Thus, we include some helpful resources to provide you with further guidance and inspiration as you continue your journey.

2

Navigating a Relationship
Before Marriage

When Sue and Tom came to see me, they had been dating on and off for over ten years. Each time they felt they had overcome a hurdle in their relationship, another one emerged. So they decided that things could not be worked out, and they dated others. But they seemed to keep coming back together. First it was the attitude of their parents that kept them apart. Then it was the talk about children: their religious upbringing and education. They wanted to talk to me about what to expect in their marriage, but they were hesitant to do so. They just didn't know how else to imagine what was ahead of them, and they hadn't yet married or had children.

All relationships take time. Anyone who has ever been in a relationship surely knows that. But what most people do not know is that interfaith relationships take more time, particularly when partners have a sense that a relationship might evolve into a long-term commitment. It is also important to acknowledge that specific decisions will have to be made (or at least that a variety of specific topics will have to be broached) years before they appear relevant to the partners' lives, even when they can't be seen emerging on the horizon. Generally, in an interfaith relationship, more significant decisions will have to be made earlier than what might be considered "normal" in an evolving relationship, maybe even before the relationship actually becomes a committed one—certainly earlier than perhaps is the case for their peers who are marrying within their own religious community. As part of their plans for the future, couples should anticipate the need to devote additional time in the years ahead to give attention to the complex details of an interfaith relationship.

Each interfaith relationship will make its own path, but some precautions can be taken in an attempt to keep it robust. People in interfaith relationships who take such precautions produce marriages most likely to succeed against tremendous odds. Many of the interfaith issues that are critical to a relationship's survival are very difficult for couples to verbalize to each other, in part because they may not have formally put them into words for themselves. This is particularly the case when figuring out how to interface with parents who may not be supportive, or in making difficult decisions about children and their religious upbringing. That's why it is important for both partners to be honest and clear about their needs and the direction they want the relationship to take. Proceeding on the assumption that you can convince your partner to change his or her position on crucial topics or feelings later means setting yourself up for a crisis. This is a mistake often made by interfaith couples who naively believe that "love conquers all."

CHOOSING TO EXPERIMENT WITH A RELATIONSHIP

Dating patterns are the direct result of where people live, where they work, and where they go to school. For some people, it is woven into the fabric of their social lives, even if they live in a community whose Jewish population is very large. Fern dated many non-Jews at her small liberal arts college. And although there were many Jews in Chicago, she seemed to meet mostly non-Jewish men at work. Since she was used to interfaith dating, she simply continued to do so. Interfaith dating is especially commonplace in small Jewish communities. A college student reminded me recently that although he wanted to marry someone who was Jewish, he had grown up as close friends—nearly family—with the few Jewish girls who were in his small Colorado town. Some people may even choose to date people of other faiths as part of a liberal approach to contemporary life. Sharon told me that while she didn't actually choose to date men of color, doing so seemed to fit her liberal political attitudes. In addition, she seemed to meet primarily black men in her work for a progressive political organization. For individuals in a less diverse community, the fact that a new date (maybe just an acquaintance) is Jewish could turn out to be a real surprise. Sammy told me that when he first started dating Nicole, she had never even met a Jewish person before. Nicole had grown up in a small rural community in the Midwest. So she took for granted that Sammy would come home with her for the holidays. She was surprised at Sammy's hesitation.

Some people are drawn to the exotic nature of dating someone who is different. One young Jewish man told me that he is attracted only to Asian and African-American women—almost all of whom are not Jewish. His attitude may be a conscious rejection of parental values or family culture, as it is with a small number of interfaith couples—something carried into the years beyond the natural rebellion of adolescence—or it may simply be based on physical and emotional attraction.

The religious upbringing or degree of current religious practice of a potential partner may seem to be irrelevant at first to one's social life or relationship, but it never really is. Even before Joan met her husband, Larry, she just assumed that everyone in her dating sphere was some type of Christian, whether lapsed or an active participant in a church. She had no experience with the Jewish community or its members, so she hadn't even considered the possibility of dating someone Jewish—that is, until her first date with Larry. So when they went out, it never occurred to her that going to a company Christmas party with a guy she had just met might develop as an interfaith relationship. She hadn't even considered it. But that is what happened.

Joan recalls having difficulty telling her best friend after her first date, "I didn't know that he was Jewish." She didn't know how her friend would respond. But then Joan's next thought was "Now *this* could be very interesting!" But no warning signal went off in her head. Why should it? She had had no experience in interfaith dating, and Larry seemed like such a nice guy! She had absolutely no idea what was ahead for both of them. Joan was a steadfast Lutheran, and she was not really on the lookout for a husband. While Larry had originally been brought up as an Orthodox Jew, his family had dropped many of the traditional ritual observances of Jewish religion. But he had maintained the cultural aspects of Judaism that often accompany such upbringings. Early in their relationship, neither Joan nor Larry had any idea about the challenges they would face together—and that they would continually revisit during the next twenty-five years of marriage.

How Might Dating This Person Affect My Future Life and Other Relationships?

Some couples give little thought to their differing religions, preferring to focus on what they have in common. The term "interfaith" may seem foreign—even irrelevant—to them. However unwanted or uncomfortable, the labels "intermarriage" and "interfaith" force couples to face issues that will be critical to developing a healthy and happy relationship, particularly when there are decisions to be made about future children as well as about relationships with parents, in-laws, and adult siblings. Personal spiritual issues may also come to the fore at different times. The labels help couples understand what they will encounter: the likely resistance of both religious communities and the families into which they are marrying, and potential negotiations over their respective spiritual needs.

If you are the Jewish partner in the relationship, you might have thought that you were brought up with a specific set of values, broadly called secular humanism, shaped by Judeo-Christian civilization and a measure of what might be termed American civil religion. And you may well see those values mirrored in your potential mate. Whether you gained those values in school or absorbed them by osmosis from the culture, your families probably interpreted them and shaped them and then called them their own. They might or might not have even thought of them as Jewish. Either way, they might have dominated the family landscape, while religion per se—the occasional visit to a service or bar mitzvah—seemed less important. That is, until you bring home a non-Jew! Indeed, many young Jews about to marry tell me that their parents expressed a sudden interest in Judaism when they—their sons and daughters—developed a serious relationship with someone who was not Jewish. Of course, there are many active Jews or those who grew up in active Jewish families who also meet and marry non-Jews. As might be expected, their families go through a great deal of inner searching as a result.

Because religion seemingly did not play a very big part in their childhood, for some people the notion of dating someone from another faith community is "no big deal." Perhaps that is because they do not consider themselves as really belonging to a particular faith community. John said to me right after he said hello, "I just don't understand what is upsetting my parents. I didn't go to Hebrew school, and I can't remember the last time my parents went to the synagogue—even for the High Holy Days." Individuals like John may view Judaism as the faith community of their parents, but it is certainly not one they claim for themselves. So the interfaith relationship may even initially be a "bigger deal" for parents than it is for either partner. Sometimes parents cling to ethnic (rather than religious) identities that are rekindled only when the prospect of someone who would "dilute" that ethnic identity wants to marry their child. Ethnic identity is probably a holdover from previous generations of immigrants whose Judaism was informed more by foods than by religion.

IS THE QUESTION OF RELIGION ON THE AGENDA NOW?

The discussion of religion seems as if it should be reserved for a "real" relationship, not merely a date for the movies or dinner. And perhaps conventional wisdom dictates that certain topics such as religion have no place in first-date conversation. But the first date is the first step to a more serious relationship. So bring the topic of religion up early in your relationship—even as early as the first date. After the birth of her first child, Simone told me that she regretted not having discussed religion and children early in her relationship with Stan. "It is so much more complicated now, and I feel much more pressured to make the right decision. I am also afraid that making the wrong decision will hurt our child and our marriage." If open and honest communication is indispensable to any successful relationship, it is even more so in interfaith relationships. You've got that many more minefields to dodge. One friend, Lori, reminded me that she had told her future husband, a new neighbor, that she could not date him because she was committed to marrying some-one who was Jewish. He kept asking her to "just have dinner," and she kept saying "I can't." But that was before they got to know each other, became close friends, started dating, and then found them-selves in love.

In raising the question of religion, you may be concerned about risking the entire relationship. Consider whether you are skewing the conversation about religion in a certain way in an attempt to protect the possibility of a future relationship. In other words, don't just listen to what you want to hear yourself—or your partner—saying, like "My religion isn't important to me." Now may also be the time to begin to explore your own religion (if your knowledge is limited, or if you left it behind as a rebellious adoles-cent), as well as the religious community of your partner (particu-larly if you have limited knowledge of it).

A second date generally means that a couple wants to pursue at least the possibility of a continued relationship. You have to recog-nize that you might have agreed to a second date for a variety of reasons. It may simply be its exotic or forbidden nature. Perhaps you may think that it is dangerous—or strictly safe, because you would "never" marry outside your religious community.

Regardless of the reasoning, be forewarned. This second date is more than a date: it could already affect your relationship with your family, since it is a step forward in an evolving relationship. (This is only in theory, however, since most parents are not aware of their adult children's second dates.) At the same time, you have to consider whether or not your parents or other family members will eventually reject the person you may choose.

This is the time to begin to honestly evaluate your situation— the one you have created for yourself, and the situation that the Jewish community has shaped for you without your consent. As the Jewish part of the couple, this may be the time to begin exploring your own feelings regarding religion. You may want to ask your partner-to-be some questions:

- How important is religion to you?
- Are you willing to learn what you do not know?
- Are you prepared to create a Jewish home with me?
- Can you respect my religious feelings?

Now ask yourself these questions:

- How important is Judaism to me personally?
- Am I willing to learn what I do not know?
- Am I prepared to take the time that will be necessary to create and maintain a Jewish home?
- Will my partner-to-be respect my religious feelings?
- Can I accept my partner's religious tendencies?
- Am I capable of trying to understand the sacrifices that my partner-to-be will make, and to acknowledge them?

It is one thing to attempt to please family members and community, but quite another to follow through on the work that will need to be done.

After you have thought through these questions, ask yourself whether you are attempting to create or force a relationship when the signs are clear that maybe you should not continue it. Make sure you are realistic and willing to face what will undoubtedly be real and unending challenges. For most couples, there is an implicit danger in marrying outside of the Jewish community. Not only will such a marriage affect your various family and social relationships, it will also help determine the choice of community in which you raise your future children. Thus, to continue the relationship is a weighty decision to make—much more so than even the serious nature required by marriage itself, particularly in an age when long-term relationships often end in divorce. When I met with a couple who had just celebrated their fifth anniversary and wanted to be of help to other couples just starting out, they told me that although they love each other and are totally committed to each other and their children, they had no idea when they were dating that their marriage would take so much work.

Relationships evolve over time, sometimes seemingly of their own accord. Some people know they're a match after a first date; in other cases, a casual relationship suddenly turns serious. Factors beyond your control can speed them up, slow them down, call time-out. The reactions of family and friends can prompt you to take a stand before you may feel ready. When you enter into an interfaith relationship, steel yourself for the unknown.

MEETING THE PARENTS AND SIBLINGS

Meet the Parents was a popular film devoted to the fear that almost everyone grapples with when they anticipate the first encounter with potential in-laws. When my wife, Sheryl, met my parents for the first time, she was a bit nervous. We went home for dinner. She carefully opened a can of grape soda that had apparently been warmed by the Florida sun—and sprayed it all over my father's white shirt and the white tablecloth that my grandmother had painstakingly crocheted.

Meeting "the folks" is considered by most people to be an indicator of future intentions. If you are not sure whether you want to proceed with the relationship, then perhaps you should not pursue it. The more your potential partner becomes a part of your family, the more difficult it will become to back out of a relationship without hurting others or yourself. Since honesty and openness are always best at the start of a relationship, it will be important to share a great deal about your family before formal introductions are made. This may be the first time you honestly face the limitations of your parents. In preparation for the visit, remember to mention to your date childhood memories that include aspects of your religious upbringing. They may be faint memories for you, but it is possible that your parents will suddenly remember every detail in order to remind you and your date of your upbringing. Be prepared for the reappearance of every photo and the recollection of each anecdote—that includes a gathering of family for a religious occasion or holiday.

For those who have a close relationship with their siblings, it is important to prepare for these encounters as well. If you don't do so, you may unknowingly drive a wedge in your relationship with your brothers or sisters—and they will blame your partner as the root cause. Similarly, you may want to meet your potential partner's siblings, particularly if they have a good relationship, before you meet your potential in-laws. This may help pave the way and help you to get a better understanding of the dynamics of your "new family" as well. Cindy likes to say that her family looks like the United Nations. Her brother married an African man, and her sister married someone from India. So when she brought home a Christian man from Omaha, Nebraska, to meet her Jewish parents, after spending some time with her siblings and their spouses, it was easy.

It is uncomfortable for most people to meet the parents of someone whom they are dating. And it may be more uncomfortable in an interfaith relationship. We tend to project our own fantasies and fears on people before we meet them. We imagine what they are going to be like because of where they live, what kind of work they do, and what religion they practice. Remember this popular wisdom: the true test of character is how you behave when you don't know what to do. That's why it is probably better to keep the first family encounter informal and to avoid a more elaborate gathering, like Grandpa's seventy-fifth birthday party. After you have created a low-stress scenario for the first meeting, the most important thing is for you to be yourself. When you meet the family, you want to make sure that "what they see is what they get." Don't be surprised if future parents-in-law ask about your plans for children and their religious upbringing. Some couples have agreed to bring their children up with two faiths so that they can decide on their own, and this can be very unsettling—if not catastrophic—for parents to hear. They will hear it as a rejection of their faith. Also, it is infrequent that children are actually brought up with two faiths. Generally, parents who have made this decision mean that they share family holiday traditions, or religious entrance or birth ceremonies, and little else. They do not consider weekly religious worship or participation in both faiths. (More about this in chapter 4.)

Couples often remember their first encounters with each other's parents. During a conversation with Jack and April, she told me, "Everything I did was wrong. My parents never had 'formal' holiday parties, so I had no idea that I would be so underdressed when I arrived to meet Jack at his parents' home—he was already there—and I was dressed in a nice dress, but everyone else was in fancy cocktail gowns and tuxedos. It was all downhill from there. I had no idea that Jack's parents had invited all of his relatives and some of their friends to meet me. I felt like I was back at my first job interview after college."

After the big meeting-of-the-parents, have a debriefing. Share your first impressions and concerns honestly but carefully. Since family relationships have greater potential for strain in an interfaith relationship than in a relationship between members of the same faith, express your concerns as objectively as possible. Your potential partner may not be ready to hear anything that may be perceived as critical of his or her parents and will need your help in doing so. Give your potential partner complete support and be encouraging. The way you help your partner with your parents now can be a model for the way you work through other things.

Even after twenty-five years of marriage, and even more years after first bringing Larry home, Joan continues to marvel at her parents' loving support as seen in their behavior toward Larry from the beginning. She says, "They let me go. They just let me go. I could feel it. It's true that I was no longer a kid, and I had been many years away from a painful broken engagement, but as steeped in Christian doctrine as they were, it took an incredible amount of love—and continually does—to let go of me and their profound vision of eternal life for me that they felt was lost in the process. They understood that *I* was the one who would have to live by my decision to marry outside the Christian faith community. In the midst of sorting out their relationship with Larry and with me, they looked for spiritual guidance, as they continue to do, and they have always encouraged me to do so, as well."

WORKING THROUGH ISSUES AS THE RELATIONSHIP EVOLVES

It is crucial that you make frequent reality checks regarding the profound degree of love, respect, and commitment that will be required for this relationship to succeed. In general, be reflective about how the relationship is progressing. Ask yourself questions like these: "Am I being honest with myself, or am I in denial? Is the headiness of infatuation affecting my better judgment?" Although it does not seem fair, an interfaith relationship requires more introspection than a marriage between two of the same religious faith. You may have to extend yourself to your partner in ways that you never anticipated at the beginning of your relationship. Consider, for example, how you may be "using" religion in your relationship. Are you forcing your partner to make concessions for the sake of religion, or forgo things dear as a result of it, when you yourself are not prepared for similar sacrifices? Do you make your partner "prove" love through religious commitments, much as sex is often used in teen dating? (For example, "If s/he loved me enough, s/he would convert.") Because religious differences can be a source of stress, they can become a source of problematic relationship patterns. Consider these concerns:

- Are you suppressing your own religious interest?

- Are you secretly disturbed by your partner's religious belief or practices while telling yourself that doesn't matter?

- Are you afraid that you will miss some of your childhood holiday memories and want to share them with your partner and, eventually, your children?

The key to a long-lasting partnership, based on a loving relationship, is honesty—with yourself and with your partner. If you are honest with each other, you will be able to deal with any challenge as a united front. According to the late Rabbi Samuel Sandmel, "The greatest hazard lies not in the openly held viewpoints in the traditions but in the more subtle areas of unexpressed emotional identification and response. A Christian can learn the factual data about Judaism or a Jew those about Christianity. But unconscious loyalties that suddenly become awakened can present surprises which not only may be unpleasant, but be disruptive of a relationship."[1]

When Sven and Sharon came to me for premarital counseling, they were frankly bewildered by Sharon's parents' behavior. Sven had been brought up in Europe as a proud atheist. Sharon had been brought up as a twice-a-year Conservative Jew in suburban New York. Her parents were delighted that she had found someone, having worried that she would remain alone the rest of her life, since she was already thirty-five when she met Sven. As the wedding plans developed, each bit of advice offered by her parents puzzled her more than the last. During Sharon's childhood, her parents had never made a big deal about being Jewish. Yet, they were now saying, "Of course, the wedding will be at a synagogue. Of course, there will be a rabbi. And, of course, when you have children [her mother meant sons], there will be a *bris.*" Sharon's only response, which she kept to herself, was "I hope we just have girls."

Questions about children top the list of tension-creating topics. Should we have them? If so, when? How many should we have? For any interfaith couple, the question "In what faith should we raise them?" is certainly the most pressing. It looms over the relationship even when it is not discussed.

Joan made the decision about raising her children as Jews early in her relationship with Larry, years before the children were born. "I knew that Larry could not raise non-Jewish children, and I knew in my heart that I wouldn't be able to stand having children who wouldn't have God in their lives. So that was the direction that I felt I had to take."

Particular circumstances, like the personal background of one partner's parents, may enter the picture. Terry was raised in a large Roman Catholic family. When her mother-in-law confided her belief that she had survived the Holocaust in order to make sure that she would bring Jewish grandchildren into the world, Terry knew that her decision about how to raise the children was made. She felt unable to convert to Judaism herself, but her children would be raised as Jews, and her home would be Jewish. She was sure of that, and fortunately she felt okay about it.

If your partner has children from a previous marriage, consider their ages, who has custody, and the added challenge of blended families before drawing any conclusions about the religious upbringing of children. Your new stepchildren may practice a different religion and live in your home. Be open to creative solutions. Step-parenting is hard enough, but when two religions are shared with two different families, it is even more difficult. This may be as disorienting for you as for the children who may come with you into your new relationship.

Rabbi Tirzah Firestone told me about a crucial decision she was once forced to make. She married a Jewish man who had children from a previous interfaith marriage. Although the children had not been raised with any particular religion, they had celebrated Christmas together as a family. The man's first wife had died while the children were quite young, and the children's only memory of their mother was associated with the Christmas tree. So this rabbi made a bold and brave decision to allow a Christmas tree in her home for the sake of her relationship with her stepchildren. She understood that sometimes a tree is just a tree and sometimes it is more than a tree. But when it becomes more than just a tree, it does not necessarily mean that it is transformed into a religious symbol. In this case, the Christian tree was a family memory, not an emblem of their religion.

COMING TO THE DECISION

The decision to marry alters your relationship with just about everyone in your family, particularly your parents, and everyone you know in your social circle. Expect some shaking up. Some people intermarry as a subconscious rejection of the parental culture in which they were raised. By choosing an interfaith relationship, you may want to "show" your parents that you are your own person. Or your parents may interpret it that way. Just when you need your family as you make difficult transitional decisions, they may not be there for you because you may have inadvertently pushed them away or because they may feel pushed.

My work with interfaith couples suggests that they develop subtle mechanisms for distancing themselves from those aspects of their family heritage—and their family—that in their own minds might jeopardize the harmony of their relationship as a couple and their day-to-day lives. They claim that certain things in religion are designed for children or really have no meaning any longer. Sometimes they physically distance themselves. So your new relationship had better be a good one, because the foundation of the family you are building is based on the strength of that relationship. As you nurture your relationship with your first family (the term sometimes used to describe one's family of origin) you will be able to nurture your new relationship as well.

For most couples, interfaith relationships take longer than other relationships to jell, to move toward becoming more permanent. Joan likes to call this pattern "the interrupted relationship." It may start and stop as the members of a couple cautiously take steps forward—maybe even breaking off for a time because of the actual or anticipated difficulties, often as a result of family or community pressure.

Other couples are drawn together. Both members know that they need to be together. There is a mutual commitment to the relationship, even to marriage, but they hesitate because of the challenges that they recognize they will face as a married couple, especially an intermarried one.

Be assured of one thing: the wedding is just one road marker along the way. Despite all the fuss that went into it and the years that led up to it, a wedding is a short ceremony—one that lasts only about fifteen minutes (okay, plus the processional, recessional, reception, and honeymoon). There is a lifetime that follows. Esther Perel, a psychotherapist in New York City who specializes in working with intermarried couples, reminds us, "All marriages entail the discovery of and discussions about differences."[2] Yours will just entail more of both. Your life together awaits you. You have plenty of time to continue to discover each other. Take the time you need, and use it wisely.

Tips

1. It's never too early to start talking about important issues and feelings. Early in your relationship, begin a discussion with your partner about what an interfaith relationship would mean to you and your families.

2. Be realistic about prospective difficulties. Interfaith relationships are seldom easy. It is important to identify challenges as they emerge—whether large or small—that will affect the stability of your relationship.

3. Be completely supportive. Because of the ongoing challenges that interfaith couples face, individuals need to support each other fully, especially in their dealings with respective family members. The trust that derives from such support creates a powerful glue for any relationship.

4. Be sensitive to your partner's point of view. Some things that emerge in a relationship aren't logical or rational, but they are just as real. As you try to figure out how to respond to each other's issues, try taking your partner's perspective, as well as that of his or her parents.

3

RELATING TO PARENTS, GRANDPARENTS, AND SIBLINGS

Every couple has numerous concurrent, sometimes conflicting, sets of relationships. The first is between the two loving partners. The second is between each partner and his or her family. Then there's the added relational layer between each partner and the other partner's family. Managing so many relationships simultaneously is a lot like juggling. In order to keep all those balls in the air—rather than letting them make a big thud by your feet—it's important to anticipate points of family conflict. You want to address tensions and differences before they become too big to do anything about. If you just ignore them and hope they'll go away, they will get bigger.

But amidst the tension that can arise between individuals and their families, everyone can also find opportunities to grow. However, parents are often afraid. They may be afraid of losing their child, their dreams for their grandchildren. Regardless of the religious background of the family—on either side—there is generally widespread ignorance about the "other" religion. And the unknown is almost always a source of fear. But the "other" can be interesting and inviting. Thus, good solid information and first-hand experiences of the "other" have the potential to correct any erroneous assumptions and bring members of the family closer together.

In general, intermarriage is better accepted today than it was in the past, as recent research indicates. This may be a result of the increased emphasis on individuals and their right to make choices in life. Most certainly it is a result of the comfort that members of the Jewish community feel about living freely in America. It is an affirmation of democracy and diversity and a reflection of upward mobility. It may also be a reflection of interethnic relationships that are displayed in the media and other images in advertising and film. This is also a time when specific intermarriages may be less accepted today, such as intermarriages between Muslims and Jews. On the other hand, multiracial marriages (which are discussed at length in chapter 9) are more accepted by the population in general.

Yet, parents still try to protect their children—even as adults—from real or imagined dangers. They understand the psychological demands of marriage, regardless of religious background. They want to protect their children from whatever would cause added marital stress. But, as Rabbi Sam Gordon, who works almost exclusively with interfaith couples in his suburban Chicago congregation, likes to say, "All marriages are intermarriages." He reminds us that most couples come from different backgrounds and must meld those backgrounds in order to form a successful union. Adding such a weighty variable as two vastly different religious backgrounds increases the potential for conflict, to be sure. But this does not mean that the couple cannot surmount these stresses. I have worked with many couples who have managed to do so.

THE RELIGIOUS VIEW OF PARENTS

If you are a parent reading this book, I encourage you to express your religious views while your children are young, and to make sure that your views reflect your behavior. Otherwise, your children will make assumptions about your feelings and religious loyalties based primarily or solely on your actions and activities (or the lack thereof). Children cannot read your mind. They will be surprised when you voice religious opinions that they haven't heard before. If you are an adult child reading this book, you may be surprised to find that your parents view your choice of a partner through the lens of a religion they don't even seem to embrace or practice. It is not uncommon for adult children to suddenly discover that they have underestimated the value placed by parents on their religious roots when they bring home their intended partner for the first time.

When Don first came to see me, he reminded me that his parents were members of a synagogue when he was younger but had dropped out after his bar mitzvah. "Religion just didn't seem important to them. Sure, they went to High Holiday services—that is, when they weren't traveling. I was just surprised at their reaction when I brought Marie home to meet them."

Just as you may want your parents to respect your decisions, you need to find a way to understand and accept your parents' feelings. This is true even when they cannot explain their feelings. Feelings about religious identity are often so elemental, so close to the core, that people have trouble putting them into words. As some disappointed parents have told me, "we just know in our bones that intermarriage is wrong."

In fact, parents may be surprised at their own reaction. They may have considered themselves too liberal or too enlightened for such feelings. In response, they may become overly emotional or subtly subversive. Adult children have often told me that their parents have said, "If you go through with *this* marriage, I will not pay for the wedding." This seems to be a popular choice of many parents who are unhappy with their children's choice of a life partner. Sometimes the approach is different. One man, Robert, shared with me his disappointment: "Once I started dating Karen, my parents' calls became less frequent. I don't know if they realized it, but I certainly did." Unless addressed directly, resolved, or at least minimized, the parents' fear of religious or cultural loss may resurface or intensify in the future. The impending birth of grandchildren often triggers the resurgence of such fears.

Jewish parents may retreat into a survival mode, sensing a danger that their roots may be lost or severely altered before they can be replanted into the next generation. This posture is especially surprising when it is taken by parents who do not actively engage Judaism, who do not go to synagogue regularly, or who may not appear to be closely connected to the Jewish community. For some, the horror of the Holocaust becomes extremely personal, even if it was not directly experienced by close family members. So the horrible words that "intermarriage is finishing Hitler's work" echo throughout many Jewish homes.

Every religious group has its own set of fears, usually stemming from its history or the collected experience of individual families. Christian parents often fear that their child or grandchildren will lose their opportunity for eternal life. Moreover, they may fear that their child's decision will relegate them to the difficult position of a vulnerable minority. Fear about hate groups lashing out at Israel and the Jewish community may also come into play. Often Christian partners don't realize that such potential stigmas are a big part of their own family's fears until they are verbalized by one family member or another. While their children may not see members of the Jewish community as a minority group, the parents may bring with them the perception of a fragile marginality from their youth. Certainly, their own experiences with prejudice colors their perspective. This may be more the case in some regions of the country than in others, particularly in small southern communities where the Jewish population may be small or nonexistent.

Parents may go to great lengths to break up an interfaith relationship and may often be urged on by others, including some religious authorities. They may, in fact, succeed—but as collateral damage they often destroy the good relations they have with their own children. After speaking publicly about this issue during a visit to a community on the West Coast, a middle-aged man approached me and confided, "That's exactly what my parents did. They forced me to break up with the only person I ever loved, and now I find it difficult to even love them. And we were very close when I was younger." After sitting for a cup of coffee, he told me the whole story—including the fact that he has not been able to find anyone to replace the woman he broke up with years before. Although parental actions may be ill-conceived or inappropriately directed, they come from what parents believe to be the right place in their hearts. They want to protect their child from what they see as a disastrous choice in his or her life. But their actions are sometimes the result of *their* embarrassment, guilt, or concern about the family's standing in the community, rather than the wishes or even the best interest of their child. Jewish community professionals and volunteer leaders are particularly and understandably most susceptible to these feelings. One Jewish educator told me, "I had to do something. I couldn't let my daughter date a non-Jewish man while I was leading the community day school."

The disappointment or scorn of a key family member, particularly a patriarch or matriarch of sorts, may be especially painful for parents. A young woman, Suzy, a successful lawyer who had lived on her own in Miami for several years, told me about hearing all the "buzzing" and veiled comments about an Aunt Sarah in her fiancé's family when she first encountered Matt's family. She didn't understand the standing of this mythical aunt until she finally went to New York to meet her future father-in-law's older sister. They talked about lots of things. Suzy sensed Sarah's approval when she told her how she had put herself through college and law school, even though her parents could have afforded it. Sarah had wanted them to save their money for their retirement and not spend it on her. After the visit, Suzy figured that she must have passed muster with Aunt Sarah. She began to notice that in almost every conversation with her new family, her future in-laws included a phrase like "Sarah just loves Suzy"—an indicator to others that "Suzy is okay."

Your Relationship with Your Partner in Light of Your Relationship with Your Parents

Tensions between you and your parents can lead to problems with your partner as well. When Stephen and I first spoke, he told me that he hadn't gotten along with his parents since his adolescent rebellion. He didn't realize that he had carried this tension into his relationship with his wife early in their marriage until she brought it to his attention. Paradoxically, difficult parents can actually strengthen the couple by being the "common enemy." Both Audra and her husband referred to her parents as "the 'rents." This was their shorthand approach for dealing with them. They were difficult people. Audra knew that they would not be supportive of anyone she married. So they worked together to work against the parents. But when one partner fails to stand up to parental pressure, that couple's ability to stand together against adversity is already weakened. Their trust has already taken a hit. Often the smallest slight made in public by a mate—an uncaring remark, a conspiratorial smirk—can feel like gross abandonment and betrayal. Couples have to be made aware of the inherent risk they face in their marriage when they let their parents come between themselves and their partners. Even when family members eventually change their attitude, it's hard to regain the trust.

Double-check your own motives for sustaining the relationship with your potential life partner. It's common to run away from a marriage that is fraught with challenges and difficulties. Stress about family relationships, finances, and children are normal to every marriage. Divorce has become a quick option that is exercised all too frequently. You must be willing to face these challenges together before you get married—and during the earlier, more difficult periods of adjustment (generally the first five years). Most adults who anticipate a lifetime commitment have some measure of doubt. It's normal. But it is important to take stock of yourself, nonetheless, and make sure that you have the personal strength to enter into this commitment. Love may conquer a great deal, but it surely does not conquer all. It may make things bearable, but few people dream of a merely bearable relationship or marriage.

Understanding your spouse's religious and cultural background is an important part of the basis for building a successful marriage. These are the memories that he or she brings into the home you will build together and may want to recreate there. So be specific, and ask about them. It will also be important background information for you as you strive to understand your new in-laws and the religious world in which they live. Even if your partner does not actively observe the family's religion, go together to a worship service of his or her religion of birth.

Read books about the other religion. Take instructional classes if that would be important to your partner. But much more than a knowledge of history and theology are needed. Be attentive. Listen carefully. And observe. Pay attention to details and nuances. Books can't offer the taste, feel, and smell of family holidays and their celebration. Books can't recapture the relationship between family members when they gather at home for a holiday celebration. What were the daily, weekly, and seasonal holiday practices of the family and of their community of friends—even when the family seemingly did not participate in them? Try to peer through the lens of the other family, not just your own.

My rule for family relationships is very simple. Each partner is responsible for dealing with challenges relevant to his or her own family members. One may be critical of one's own family members, but that right is not given to one's partner. Let your partner alone criticize his or her own side of the family!

If you are rejected by your partner's parents, try not to take it personally. On the other hand, don't deceive yourself into believing that genuine friendliness is a sign of total acceptance. True acceptance is a generous and intimate gesture that takes time, like most other aspects of an interfaith relationship.

Non-Jews in particular see the practice of religion as linked to a particular religious institution. For many, religion is centered on the church or other place of worship. They find curious the home-based religion of Jews who may not participate in the activities of the synagogue. Joan, for example, was surprised to see such a deep commitment to Judaism expressed by Larry and his family despite their infrequent attendance at synagogue. She quickly learned that there is not always a direct correlation between church and synagogue attendance and the requisite commitment to the religious community. Even synagogue membership doesn't correlate with prayerfulness. There is a long continuum of personal religious practice that is not necessarily reflected in commitment to a Jewish institution.

Similarly, as the Jewish spouse, you may not understand your partner's family's religious involvement. They may, for example, have elaborate Christmas and Easter celebrations without necessarily belonging to a church. Or they may engage in Buddhist practice and yet not be associated with an ashram.

Avoid using your own religion or your family's religious practice as a measuring stick. Joan tells me that she worries most when the Jewish partner in a couple seems to underestimate a partner's connection to the religion or culture of his or her family. Perhaps Jews tend to do this more than others, as a result of their own ambivalent connections to Jewish religion. The fact is that people generally underestimate their ties to their family's religion. Many intermarried individuals have admitted to me that religious beliefs learned in childhood and other cultural aspects of their partner's life were far more embedded than they anticipated. People do not intend to mislead their partners about their religious commitment. They just don't realize its magnitude.

Two skills will serve you best: attentive listening and observing. Joan says that after so many years of marriage, she still relies on her mother's early advice, which has worked well: "Keep your mouth closed, and watch what everyone else is doing." (Keeping one's mouth shut, she muses, remains the most difficult!) Perhaps she was overstating her warning. But it is indeed better to be silent and observe. Then you can ask questions. As for your mate's entry into the Jewish world, beware: Family members (usually acting as stereotypical "Jewish in-laws" to your partner) become sudden authorities on Judaism and Jewish life, even when—or rather especially when—their knowledge may be severely limited. It may be what they observed or remember from childhood. What they think is generally interpreted as "*the* way of Judaism." Any disagreement may be seen as an attempt to undermine their foundational beliefs. Make sure that these are not your or your partner's only windows into Jewish life. This is particularly important if your partner has embarked on a personal course of study of Judaism.

I generally recommend that couples take classes together—something often encouraged by rabbis and others in the Jewish community. This provides an important common foundation of knowledge and information, as well as a point of departure for discussions. It gives you a vocabulary with which to address your concerns. Finally, it introduces you to others with similar questions and experiences. It's easier to bring up sensitive topics and ask what may seem to be obvious questions when you know you are not alone. While your partner may be anxious, you can assure her that those leading the classes—whether they are rabbis or volunteer leaders—take special care to make such classes inclusive and nonthreatening. One participant in an Introduction to Judaism class told me, "I thought that I had 'shiksa' written all over me and that alarms would go off as soon as I entered the synagogue."

It is important that you and your partner together learn from individuals who can be objective about your relationship. Beyond classes, join with others in your neighborhood, in your community, and in your workplace to share your experiences and the challenges that you will undoubtedly continue to face. The support you get from these fellow travelers will help. You may find that others have worked things out in different ways and that you can benefit from their experience and perspective.

THE DYNAMICS OF FAMILY LIFE

Family life is not static. It is constantly in motion. Similarly, neither religious life nor religious identity stays at the same pitch of intensity. Your own spiritual journey, as well as that of your partner, will undoubtedly follow a circuitous route. Then, your efforts to understand and explore will add spiritual depth to your lives and that of your family. With interfaith marriage, it is not uncommon for partners to become more observant, involved, or connected.

It may be a long time before you and your spouse are accepted by your family—if such acceptance ever fully comes. Your parents and siblings may not be able to get beyond mere tolerance. Take very good care of each other. Your marriage will be strengthened as a result, and your family will appreciate it, too. Parents want their children to be well cared for and happy, even when they do not agree with their life decisions. Parents take note of a good relationship and respect it, even if they had not planned to do so. (The blessing of grandchildren may also help!)

I asked Paul, a man in his late twenties who met his wife during a social function sponsored by the corporation for which they both worked, "What has helped you most in learning to live in and with Molly's family?" Hers was a large, well-educated, extended, well-connected Jewish family. He replied, "Realizing how much fear there was of the possibility of being swallowed up by the non-Jewish world, I began to see what was driving some of their attitudes and feelings." Sometimes understanding is all it takes. One colleague likes to talk of "the view from the balcony." From above, the spectacle of people dancing together in a crowded room looks a lot different than it does when you are a couple on the dance floor. The perspective on Jewish continuity is vastly different when you look at other families than when you consider it solely from your own viewpoint.

The concept of forgiveness calls up an extremely important value. Perhaps forgiveness is best understood as acceptance and understanding. Forgiveness is directly related to the concept of repentance, of turning in a different direction, of saying "I'm sorry" and moving forward. Forgiveness is not about waiting for someone to apologize for what he or she has said or done. It is about taking the step forward and relieving the other of his or her burden (often disarming the other as a result). In many families, countless hurtful words and deeds have been exchanged as a result of the marital decisions their children have made. No matter how hurtful an event or how much pain has been caused by something said or done, forgiveness is still possible. Danny told me that it wasn't until his father was in his late eighties that he felt able to forgive him for the pain he had caused. But years later, now that his father is gone, he feels that he did the right thing. He only wished that he had done it sooner so that his father could have had more time to spend with his grandchildren. Perhaps now is the time to forgive your parents, your siblings, your grandparents, and yourself—and ask them to do the same.

Tips

1. Ask for help. Marriage is complicated by an interfaith relationship. Others have experienced many of the challenges that you are just beginning to face. Take advantage of their experiences and the various approaches they have undertaken.

2. Don't withdraw from your family. Religion is more about family than about theology. Even though it may seem that most of the stress in your interfaith relationship is a result of family, strengthening your ties to family will provide you with the secure foundation you need as you navigate your future with your partner. In other words, stay connected even when it's hard.

3. Help your spouse stay connected. As your relationship matures, it may be difficult to stay connected with family members and friends. Just as it is important for you to maintain a relationship with your family (parents and siblings), it is important that you support your partner in his or her connection to family—even when it demands quiet sacrifice on your part.

4

Making Decisions about Children

In an interfaith relationship, it is never too early to talk about children. Bear in mind that as your relationship with your partner evolves, the decisions you initially make regarding the upbringing of children—even the decision to have them—will change in content and degree, as well. Because of this, you need to check with each other about this. Unfulfilled expectations are sure to cause problems. Too often I have heard a parent say, "But she promised that we could raise Jewish kids," only to find that the partner's views had changed without the other's knowledge.

Recently, a woman only weeks away from giving birth came to see me. She was afraid to tell her husband what she had learned from her physician just that day: she was expecting a boy. She hesitated, because he had casually mentioned only the previous day that if they were to have a son, "I really don't want him to be circumcised. It is rather barbaric, after all." This little detail had previously not surfaced. When they married and he agreed to raise their future children as Jews, she took it to mean including a ritual circumcision should they have a son. Yes, they spoke ahead of time, but certainly not enough.

A decision about how to raise children must be mutual, or it will return to haunt those involved. When I met with a group of college kids who had been raised in interfaith families, several of them didn't know whether to consider themselves Christians or Jews. They told me that they had received mixed messages from their parents and felt a great deal of resentment as a result. When I pressed one young woman, she confessed, "Now that I am at college, and able to really make my own decisions, I realize that I was caught in the midst of my parents' inability to make religious decisions for my sisters and me and stick with those decisions."

Rabbi Rachel Cowan, who is responsible for the Jewish Life program at the Nathan Cummings Foundation and who ran workshops for intermarried couples, often remarks that many couples who attended her workshops hoped that she would give them the answers to all their questions. Even if there were pat answers, she refused to do so, preferring not to rob them of the need to struggle through the questions and their resolutions. However, she is quick to point out that most of the Jewish partners in her workshops wanted to raise Jewish children. After all, that was one reason they attended the workshop in the first place. They also did not want to be unfair to their non-Jewish spouses. However, non-Jewish spouses were baffled by why it was so important to their Jewish partners to raise Jewish kids when they did not seem in any way religious. They hoped that Rabbi Cowan would tell them the "right way." The non-Jewish partner may even feel pressured early in a relationship "to raise children as Jews," since it is a requirement held by some of the rabbis who agree to officiate at interfaith marriages. Fulfilling a promise, however, is much more difficult than making one.

My advice: Make a decision before considering conception, or certainly before your child is born, and then take responsibility for your decision jointly with your partner. But it is not only Jewish parents who worry about making children Jewish. I asked Ellen, who comes from a practicing Roman Catholic family, when she had made the weighty decision to agree to raise her children as Jews. She told me that she actually made it on her own, before she and her husband talked about it. He had not wanted to force her to do anything in their relationship that might be against her conscience. Similar to what Terry experienced in making the decision to raise her children in a Jewish home, Ellen's mother-in-law, a Holocaust survivor, told her that what kept her alive through the war years was the commitment to bringing Jewish children and grandchildren into this world, and Ellen felt called to that responsibility. Her siblings could carry on the Roman Catholic traditions of her birth family; she felt that she had a more profound obligation.

Don't just say, "We'll wait and let our kids decide later." This is a cop-out. Those whose parents have said that they would let their children decide when they are older often report feeling cheated when they see their peers identify with a specific religious group, connect more with one set of grandparents or the other, or embrace one heritage. A link to a specific community will benefit your children wherever life takes them. You aren't forcing their future adult decision if you provide them with experiences and give them information, but you will force a decision if you don't. Many decisions we may make for our children when they are young are often "unmade" by our children when they become older. Since religion is more about family than it is about theology, the most important part of your children's religious upbringing may be the message that their parents have a unified position regarding their religion. Religious choices made by children when they are older are more often choices that children feel pushed to make between one parent or the other, rather than between religions. And if children perceive that it is organized religion that drives a wedge between their parents, they may opt out of formal religion entirely, regardless of the choices with which they were presented.

MAKING DECISIONS EARLY

It is critical to begin the discussion about children before marriage, making sure that there is room for flexibility once the children are born. The reality of birth often offers an added perspective. As colleague Rabbi Lance Sussman, who is blessed with five children, says, "Kids are no big deal. They just change your whole life." The decisions that have to be made about children are too important and come too quickly to be left to the already overwhelming time of birth. Traditional Jewish law requires a *brit milah* (ritual ceremony of circumcision) for a boy on the eighth day after his entrance into life. Those eight days are not long enough to enable parents to wrestle with important decisions such as circumcision. The point is that everything is possible in a mutually supportive relationship, and little in a deteriorating one—so make decisions together and early, and talk about them often.

TAKING RESPONSIBILITY FOR RAISING YOUR JEWISH CHILDREN

Jewish education is not about compensating for experiences you can't provide yourself; it's about building Jewish memories. Jack, a managing attorney in a major law firm in the East and president of a local Jewish community center, told me that his intermarriage had made him a better Jew and a better Jewish parent. This was initially puzzling until Jack explained, "Before we were married, we made a decision to raise the kids Jewishly. I knew then that it would be my responsibility, since Susan knew nothing about Judaism. If Judaism was important to me—and it is—then I would have to learn before I could teach my children. So once the children were born, I was in a much better position to teach them. And I continued to learn. And so, by the way, did Susan." He took courses. He studied on his own. He took advantage of nearly every opportunity in his community to increase his base of Jewish knowledge.

Joan had heard that Rabbi Monty Syme and members of his synagogue in suburban Detroit were welcoming to interfaith couples. During their first conversation, Rabbi Syme told Joan that she had a responsibility to provide Jewish experiences for her children. It was up to her to figure out what those experiences would be. So she translated her religious upbringing into a Jewish context. She made elaborate Shabbat meals and festive holiday celebrations. Passover became a holiday extravaganza during the entire week, not just for the *seder*. Joan decorated the house extensively for holidays throughout the year. Each holiday, however minor, was observed to its fullest—in the context of family rather than strict ritual. It was the power of the religious experience that she could offer her children that mirrored Joan's own religious upbringing as a child.

If decisions are made honestly and in good faith, they can be accomplished with few regrets or ill feelings. Joan reminds us, "The day my husband put our oldest daughter in the car and I saw them leave the driveway for her first day of Hebrew school, it was admittedly one of the darkest times of my life. I knew that from that day on things would never be the same between us and that there would be a huge piece of me that she would never know or understand. I only hoped that the faith that had led me to my decision would give her the strength she would need for her to have a fulfilling life as a Jew. It has, and I thank God for my strength of faith and for hers."

If you have made a decision to raise your children as Jews, it is up to you to provide them with opportunities to affirm the identity you have chosen for them. It *does* "take a village to raise a child." This means that we need the help of our families, neighbors, relatives, and friends. Since interfaith families live in communities of various sizes, it is especially crucial to offer Jewish experiences if you are isolated from the mainstream of Jewish life. Offering them a label that has no content may even be counterproductive. Children, like adults, need to know what it means when they say, "Yes, I am Jewish."

Naomi, now in college, tells me that she resents her parents' unwillingness to stand up to her tantrums when she was five and refused to continue going to religious school. "Look at all I missed," she laments, anger rising in her voice. "And look at the education you saddled me with. You made sure that I went to the best private schools and encouraged me to attend an Ivy League college, but when it came to my religious education, you were ambivalent at best."

Joan often muses about her own children. "Our kids don't truly fit into either family well, neither Larry's nor mine. They have a very special connection to each of their grandparents, but they don't relate to them the same way their cousins do—on either side of the family. They simply lack many common experiences. They are cherished—but it is in a different way. I may be a bit wistful about it, but I have no regrets or misgivings. That's just how it is. In the case of my own parents, particularly since our kids are Jewish and my parents are not, they have always had to consciously work at their relationship with their grandchildren just a little bit harder than did Larry's parents, and we all recognize the incredible efforts they have made."

Joan realized that she had after all been successful when her close friend Julie said, "Don and I are both Jewish, and our son has no interest in Judaism at all. But look at you—you have not even converted, and you have two religious kids." But Joan reminds us, "It didn't just happen. It was part of the religious war I have been waging since the kids were born. God and religion were always important to me. It wasn't until I married Larry that Jewish religion became so important."

This is what I have learned: Mixed-marriage households often emerge much more observant than the childhood home of the Jewish spouse—that is, when both parents have made a mutual commitment to provide that environment for their kids.

Many interfaith marriages are *re*marriages, which only adds bulk to the family baggage. It is now common knowledge that what was once (perhaps inappropriately) called the normative or traditional family now represents the minority of family configurations in North America. We used to joke about the traditional family having a husband and wife, two kids (one boy, one girl), a station wagon, and a dog—living in a house with a white picket fence in suburbia. Today, it is quite common for children from one set of parents to find themselves living in a different family structure, usually with a stepmother or stepfather and often with new siblings from previous marriages. As a community, we have an obligation to affirm these family structures and the members of the families in them. Different religious issues—schools, youth groups, life-cycle events, and dietary customs—will inevitably heighten blended family concerns. At the same time, blended family issues—dual custody, the addition of stepbrothers and stepsisters, and new babies—complicate different religious issues.

Parents immersed in their own joy or their own troubles may not recognize their children's interreligious family troubles. Joan, who often counsels interfaith couples at her own congregation, once assisted at a wedding in which the bride and the groom each had a twelve-year-old daughter from a previous marriage. The parents were so absorbed in their own new love that they did not take into account how hard it was for their children to get accustomed to new stepparents, especially new-religion ones. One girl was studying for her bat mitzvah in a Conservative synagogue, while her new Christian stepsister was active in the local Methodist church. The girls chatted with Joan and sadly understood that they had no choice; there had been no room for dissent or discussion. The girls had felt forced to please their parents. They needed to get along personally, and each needed to maintain her own religion by adhering to the religion of the home where she mainly lived.

Sometimes the previous marriage was also an intermarriage. Therefore, lots of religions may be going on simultaneously. The children may participate in one religion, or they may have no religious training at all. Sometimes, the custodial parent is also the parent who directs the religious upbringing of the child. Custody may determine religion by default. In other words, children may be in a position of choosing whom to live with and choosing a religion at the same time, without necessarily realizing that they are making such simultaneous decisions. In the case of second marriages with children, just as is the case with first marriages when there are no children, it is important to talk about children early in the relationship, make decisions together, and present a united front.

It is possible to preserve a child's religion even when a second marriage brings a new religion into the home. Joan worked with one mother who continued to take her two children to Hebrew school twice a week while her new husband attended church services and events with his Presbyterian children. They celebrated the holidays of both faiths in the home together. The children were at least ten years old at the time of the second marriage and had a good foundation in their respective faiths, but the parents' commitment gave the children the support they needed to maintain their individual religious identities.

Measuring Success

We can guide our children, but ultimately they make their own decisions. One day Joan realized something we all realize about our children that is particularly important in the context of an interfaith marriage. "I realized that I was no longer in control of my children's religion. They had gone on without either of us. With or without Larry or me, we had two Jewish kids." Joan and Larry had created a Jewish home, but the kids made their own decision to affirm their upbringing.

After a conversation with the Methodist husband of a woman from a prominent Jewish family, I overheard a teacher commend him for allowing his son to be raised a Jew and not force him to make the decision between two religions by himself when he is older. This man's insight about children taught me a great deal. He remarked, "Oh, he will choose for himself, but my wife just wants to make sure he has the tools he needs to make the decision to be a Jew."

Children constantly surprise us with the choices they make, even when we plot out a specific religious life course for them. Success basically means that they have found their own way—the path that best suits their way of life—using the tools we have given them. When children make careful, deliberate religious choices, they are actually modeling what we have done for ourselves. Even those of us who walk in the religious path of our ancestors have made a conscious choice not to leave. No matter how much effort we put into generating religious experiences for our children, they will eventually take on the responsibility to navigate their own religious journey.

Giving them this freedom is not only hard for adults. It is also hard for their children. Joan recalls the day she told Sarah, her oldest daughter, that Joan was not Jewish. "She was about three. We were wrapping Hanukkah and Christmas gifts for the whole family. There was a look of fear on her face, as if to say, 'How will that fact separate us?'" Sarah somehow knew that the fact that her mom was not Jewish never affected her own sense of being Jewish. One young friend in their play group once asked her, "Are you half-Jewish because your mom is Christian?" Sarah replied, "I am not half-anything. I am Jewish." Such questions have always helped her to chart her own religious course for her life.

As our choices were different from our parents', so our children's may be too. Similarly, the world around us has changed drastically and will continue to change. The notion of an interfaith family, once radical, has become commonplace. Nevertheless, as the Jewish spouse, you want your children to be Jewish in the same way you are, even if the circumstances are considerably different. Rather than attempting to recreate a previous reality, we have to create new ones. With young children, the goal is simple: give them religious memories that provide a rudder so they can sail—steering, accelerating, catching the wind—on their own as we let go and they grow and mature. As a parent, your job is to maximize Jewish feeling in your children's world, not to manage your children's future, because you really don't have the ability to do that.

Tips

1. Make decisions about children early and mutually, and keep the dialogue going.

2. Develop your own religious identity even as you are guiding the development of your children's. Providing a Jewish environment depends in part on your own knowledge and your community connection.

3. Decide what you believe is best for your children. Don't measure success by the choices that others have made.

5

The Holidays and What to Do about Them

Holidays can form the core of an interfaith couple's life together. Religious holidays offer a structure; yet, there's room for creativity in how you choose to celebrate and make the occasion special. Also, the holidays themselves provide lessons about harmony, hope, and intercultural tolerance that interfaith couples can apply to their own lives. Most of them are joyous celebrations of the history of the Jewish people and our relationship to God and the land of Israel. The more somber holidays, like Yom Kippur, encourage personal reflection and spirituality. Holidays help bring religion to life. As a result, they also serve as connections to past and future generations. Today's celebrations are tomorrow's memories.

Research conducted by the Jewish Outreach Institute suggests that the primary portal for interfaith families into Jewish community life, particularly those families with young children, is the celebration of holidays. The holiday patterns that you develop early in your marriage will set the tone for your family life, although they will change somewhat with the birth of children, and they will evolve as you all grow and mature together.

Celebrating holidays as a family is the key ingredient in building a religious identity. Religious education is not just about schools and the transmission of information from teacher to student. Rather, religious education is about *the creating of memories.* And the most vivid religious memories are usually those that are associated with a holiday celebration—days that stick out as Technicolor in a child's mind. This does not stop when you become an adult. So you want to make sure that your memories—and those of your children—are positive, not half-hearted or begrudged.

Joan prepared her first *seder* long before her children were born—in fact, before she and Larry were married, as a surprise to him. The *seder* came from a book she found in the local public library. The book contained the *haggadah* and ingredients for the *seder* plate, but she still laughs at the meal she prepared (the guidance for which was lacking in that particular resource). It consisted of heated corned beef slices, applesauce, and potato pancakes out of a box. That was "Jewish enough," right? It wasn't until later in their relationship that she learned that "kosher *for Passover*" meant something specific—and very different from what she had prepared. Her future husband, who always kept a Passover diet, expressed delight and never mentioned the unusual menu. Later, Larry helped her learn the Passover routine and what would be necessary for their kids to have memorable, but more appropriate and extremely delicious, annual *seder* experiences. On another occasion, Joan and Larry visited Larry's elderly aunt, who kept a kosher home. She delighted in sharing family recipes with Joan to help her learn. But Joan remembers with embarrassment asking whether the pie crusts she was making, which tasted similar to her own grandmother's, were made with lard—not a kosher ingredient, to be sure!

THE CONTINUUM OF HOLIDAY OBSERVANCE: LIBERAL TO TRADITIONAL, SECULAR TO RELIGIOUS

The religious observance of holidays can best be described as following a continuum. Approaches vary depending on the degree of family practice, community custom, and the identification with a particular religious movement. While no family can totally replicate the holiday observances of their own childhoods, they can intentionally develop meaningful family observances of their own.

Find your own place to start on the continuum. Begin simply. A holiday can be marked as easily as moving a family holiday meal from the kitchen into the dining room. Choose recipes and foods that are reflective of the holiday. Bookstores are filled with helpful cookbooks and holiday resources, as is the Web. For Joan, no holiday meal would be complete without a recipe from the local synagogue cookbook. She recommends such cookbooks, because they usually also contain background about the holidays and guidance for home observance. With a little preplanning and self-initiated study, you can easily and quickly prepare an appropriate holiday meal.

Consider what the holidays mean to you. Look at various aspects of most holiday observances: historical significance, activities, music, and, of course, food. That is what Joan did. "You know you are beginning to see the world through Jewish eyes when your senses begin to react to the mention of brisket; when Friday night candle-lighting seems mysterious and special; when your Friday night table seems naked without flowers; when you can tell just how hard to press the *matzah* ball dough with your fingers so that your *matzah* balls are not tough but light and acceptable to a table of Jews of many generations; and when you are invited to a friend's home for a holiday dinner and they ask *you* to bring the chicken soup." She found that holidays are about the caring and nurturing of those you love. She also learned that building anticipation through preparation heightens the holiday experience. So she spends a lot of time shopping for just the right items, decorates the house, plays holiday-related music, and buys holiday books and cookbooks.

OPPORTUNITIES TO RESOLVE CONFLICT PRESENTED BY HOLIDAYS

While holidays present us with opportunities, they are also potential flashpoints for interfaith families. Holidays are a challenge to many new families, regardless of religious backgrounds. This is even more so the case with interfaith families. It's possible to find a comfort level, but this may take many years. Resentment and tensions can bubble up even after the main areas of conflict have been negotiated and even resolved. The ever-present acknowledgment of the "holiday season" seems to be what causes Jewish parents to revisit their feelings of discomfort with the intermarriage of their children. Christmas becomes the centrifugal force around which many tensions arise, even when there is no tree or exchange of presents.

Just as holidays may bring attention to conflicts in the marital relationship of a couple, they can also magnify problems within an extended family. These may not be about the holiday per se, but the event sets the stage. Often children leave their parents' home with many parent-child conflicts unresolved. The celebration of holidays may reignite conflict by bringing the differences between parents and their children's choices, particularly the choice of a spouse, into sharp relief. Likewise, relationships between once-close siblings may change with these choices, particularly religious ones.

More challenging is the way holidays highlight religious differences within members of the interfaith couple itself. Cultural and religious differences, dormant for months, rise to the surface around holiday time. Holidays pose questions of family loyalty. Adult children may feel caught between their relationship with the family into which they were born and the family into which they have married. For example, in interfaith marriages, more so than in-faith marriages, if you choose to celebrate a holiday with your spouse's family your own parents may question your family loyalty as a result!

Holidays can heighten feelings about personal insecurity and inferiority. Not all families are as welcoming as others to new members. Some may make newcomers feel positively inadequate. Joel and Gwen came to see me after the first time Gwen had met Joel's parents. They invited them both for a Friday night Shabbat meal. While Gwen didn't really know much about Shabbat meals, she had read a little and had discussed with Joel what to anticipate. But it made her feel incompetent when Joel's parents narrated the home ritual as if Gwen were a first-grader. When the new family member knows little about the practice of the new family's religion and holidays, insecurity and discomfort intensify. As a result, conflicts arise, and spouses are unwilling to participate in the holiday celebrations of their new families. This often leads to marital conflict as well.

Couples often take great pains to avoid the holiday question by simply opting out of making a decision. However, putting off the issue only makes it loom larger. Each time the questions about holidays and family return, with the inexorable progress of the calendar, they will become more difficult to resolve.

Sometimes we let geography make our decisions for us. We may gravitate to whichever family is closer, regardless of the religious decisions we have made. But that lets us off the hook too easily. With the choice of holiday celebrations—not just which holidays but, more importantly, with whom we celebrate them—it is common for one set of parents to read each decision that their children make as winning or losing. "If our kids celebrate with my in-laws, then I've lost."

While religious observances may conflict, you needn't surrender to conflict. Even extremely observant families from two different religions do not have to enter into conflict during the Easter/Passover season. Some measure of stress may be inevitable, but it can be reduced and channeled without one or both of you forgoing holidays altogether. Here are some ways.

Option One: Celebrate Separately

On the upside: this minimizes the chance for conflict. On the downside: it minimizes the chances for rapprochement between family members from either side. In addition, there's double the work and double the logistics. Everyone likes to try to avert conflict, especially with parents, even at the cost of avoiding them altogether. Some years ago, one of Joan's neighbors, a deeply observant Roman Catholic woman, told Joan that her son was about to marry a "very nice Jewish girl." The neighbor was somewhat resigned about it. Though brokenhearted that her son was not marrying a woman of her faith, she was delighted that he, at nearly thirty, was finally getting married. She tried desperately to hide her discontent about the bride's religion, particularly to Joan. At the end of the conversation, Joan quipped, "Well, at least you'll know that Peter will be at *your* house for Christmas and Easter," thinking that this couple could at least avoid the perennial question that young Christian newlyweds usually face: "With whose parents do we spend the holidays?" Some months later, the neighbor called to chide Joan about how wrong she had been: The couple had decided to go to Spain for Christmas.

Option Two: Celebrate Together, but Guardedly

You can include lots of neutral friends as buffers. However, family members may decide to ignore the outsiders and take advantage of the presence of an audience in order to vent whatever is on their mind, particularly things that have been kept bottled up and brewing inside for some time. Some families choose to celebrate in public places, like a park or a restaurant, hoping that everyone will be on good behavior in public. Others choose more private places, just in case.

Option Three: Celebrate Together

This demands a great deal of preparation and negotiation on both sides. Family members must try to be open and accepting of one another, regardless of their perceived religious and cultural differences. There is no clear-cut approach to celebrating together that will work for all families. But one simple rule is that *talking* about things *works,* and not talking about things does not work. Avoid contriving, but do plan ahead. Luck is the result of hard work. Knowing what to watch out for and getting advice—from this book and other sources—will help, but your own best answer will come from within your own family.

Strategies for Finding a Way That Works for Your Family

Begin by managing expectations. Most people do not intentionally say or do things to be purposely hurtful, but certain family members do have a way of pushing just the right buttons. If you expect perfect smoothness and things get rough, you'll be disappointed. Better to anticipate some trouble and perhaps be pleasantly surprised.

Consider your own attitude before being so quick to criticize someone else's. Exploring your newfound devotion to your own holidays will help you understand whatever ultimatums you may hear yourself or others making. Don't disparage either family to the other. Such comments may suddenly become public when you are all together. Be part of the attempt to bring people together, rather than stirring dissension among family members. If we are honest with ourselves, we may be entering the situation with unrealistic expectations that in themselves set us up for failure. We expect that others are not open to compromise, but really we ourselves are not.

Try to get some perspective on the situation. As Joan's grandmother used to say, "You wouldn't worry so much about what people thought of you if you realized how infrequently they did it." Extended family gatherings are not solely focused on you, your spouse, and your children. Others can make this harder or easier, but you have to take on the responsibility of finding a comfortable place for yourself. Study the holiday customs of your spouse's family. Ask your partner and your friends about their family customs and practices. Learn several holiday recipes, and perfect them to become famous among family and friends. The key to your in-laws' hearts may be their stomachs!

Be sure to demonstrate interest in your spouse's family and their holiday traditions and celebrations. Passivity may be perceived as disinterest or disdain. Don't hide in the TV room all day, even if half of the other relatives are there. As an interfaith couple, you and your family will be measured differently. As any holiday approaches, remember your secret shield against the outside world: devotion to your mate. Your caring attitude, whether articulated or demonstrated, will endear you to the family and help short-circuit the many instances of selfishness, pettiness, or pride of other members of your partner's family that may get in the way of your relationship. Always be on the lookout for supporters and mentors in the family and in the community. They will affirm your efforts and clue you in to what you need to know.

It is important to note that American culture has unintentionally absorbed the celebration of Christian culture into what might be best described as American civil religion. While this angers many Jews and may even be threatening, many Christian families are not as sensitive to this. Often, Jewish people are placed in the position of participating in holiday celebrations in schools and workplaces. There may be a feeling of "Hey, we already celebrate your holiday." This backdrop may exacerbate the challenges that interfaith families face.

GENDER ROLES

Gender roles, whether traditional or whether "reversed" or egalitarian, can have a disproportionate impact at holiday times. If one spouse tends to take care of everything and that happens to be the non-Jew in an interfaith marriage, there's the added burden of learning all the traditions and how-tos. But it can be done.

When your spouse takes on the roles of social secretary, cook, decorator, or house cleaner, make sure that you express your appreciation. As one interfaith partner told me, "I enjoy cooking and entertaining anyway, but my interest in adding Jewish recipes and staging Jewish social events at our house worked very well as an entrée into my husband's cultural world. His enthusiasm for my efforts has always given me great joy. There have been times, however, when his level of appreciation and attention did not meet my expectations. I worked hard to make the best chicken soup in town, but it hurt when he said that it was nothing compared to the way his grandmother used to make it for him when he was a child."

Be sure your partner realizes you will need support for any compromises and changes you are going to make. Protecting yourself is part of working with your spouse. As you approach your two families, it is important for couples to make decisions together and to communicate those decisions privately, ahead of time.

Most partners who come from another religious tradition enter Jewish families with the erroneous assumption that their Jewish partners have adequate knowledge about holidays. Unfortunately, many Jews are relatively uninformed about the history, development, and practices of the holidays. Thus, you will have an opportunity to find out together.

Be patient with yourself and with your partner; it takes time to "own" a new culture and its content and call them your own. There is a limit to how much learning can take place in a classroom or through solitary hours with books. Learning about holidays takes place best in their exploration and experience, even if elementary and filled with "errors." These become important parts of the family's collective memory, too. One young mother told me that her creativity with noodle kugel became legend. She tried all kinds of recipes. Like every good cook, as she gained confidence she experimented a great deal on her own, mixing a bit of her Irish background in with the noodles. But some things just don't work with kugel, and her husband and children begged her to stop and just make the kugel recipe that her mother-in-law was famous for. Don't worry about making mistakes in front of your kids. Mistakes make parents that much more human. And besides, most assume that their family's way is what everyone does. In the broad spectrum of holiday customs, it is possible that there is no right or wrong way. Joan uses this question to remind herself: "Should *matzah* balls be fluffy or chewy?" The answer: "Whichever way your grandmother made them!"

Seek out resources to help you learn. Material previously taken lightly, such as holiday booklets brought home by children from Hebrew school, and synagogue sisterhood recipe books, can become indispensable to your learning. And if your children attend Hebrew school, take part in their learning. Regardless of your religious background, there is always a need for volunteer help. If the synagogue is welcoming and supportive, synagogue participation can be a very important form of support for the intermarried family. It offers the opportunity to learn and celebrate without any additional family baggage. The connections with the synagogue can help deepen your partner's comfort zone; celebrating holidays and entering into another religious community are also about feeling comfortable in its culture and in its religious institutions. As the Jewish partner, you may have to take on the responsibility for acting as a guide, even if it entails study on your part. If you don't, you abdicate your role in the holiday. Joan has overheard this phrase spoken by many non-Jews in interfaith relationships: "Who is the Jew around here, anyway?"

WHICH HOLIDAYS TO CELEBRATE?

For interfaith couples and their extended families, perhaps Thanksgiving is an appropriate place to start. According to the Pilgrims' testimony, Thanksgiving takes its lead from the biblical celebration of Sukkot, a fall harvest festival that combines an expression of gratitude for a bountiful harvest with the remembrance of the Israelites' nomadic life as they made their way in the desert from Egyptian slavery to the promise of freedom in Canaan. Because of its American roots and subsequent secularization, Thanksgiving can speak to both partners. Because it is not overtly Christian, Thanksgiving is accessible to Jews in ways that national—but essentially Christian—holidays such as Christmas and Easter are not. In Joan's family, Thanksgiving is always celebrated at her home. Her husband's extended family joins Joan, Larry, and the girls, as do Joan's parents and her sister's family of six. And they all make sure that their celebration is more than just one side of the family "making nice" with the other. This approach grew out of their attempt to divide the secular holidays between family members. Thanksgiving seemed perfect for the Jewish branch of the family.

They join Joan's parents in *their* observance of Easter and Joan's sister's family in *their* observance of Christmas. Any vestiges of Santa

Claus and the Easter bunny have disappeared from Joan and Larry's home. Joan gave up the customs of her childhood and adopted Larry's as her own. When someone invited her to church, Joan realized that she couldn't go any more; it was too painful to be reminded that she was no longer part of that world. So Thanksgiving is a neutral time to host her Christian family in their Jewish home, and they spend Jewish holidays with their "surrogate family" of close, local friends.

While Thanksgiving may seem the perfect holiday to experiment with blended traditions, it still presents challenges. Every family has its own traditions. If your family has identified Jewishly, this relatively neutral celebration may be the time to let some of the other family's traditions come to the fore, even if they can be read as part of one religion's culture. Joan recalls the first Thanksgiving spent at their new home with family members. She had grown up in a Lutheran family that wouldn't even touch a carrot stick without a blessing. Larry, on the other hand, had shelved his Orthodox upbringing many years earlier. And his family generally began meals without prayers of blessing or gratitude. So together they adapted: Joan's habit of saying a blessing before eating emerged into using blessings within Jewish tradition. But as her relatives would be present for the Thanksgiving meal, the Hebrew would certainly be foreign to them. Joan wondered: Could this be the one time that they acknowledged *her* past by using her childhood grace? She realized, however, that her past no longer fit her present. With Larry's support, she composed a prayer that she writes each year and to which each child and adult has contributed. This is her way of bridging the disparate traditions of family members. The new tradition has been a part of the household every year, even with the snickers of newcomers or guests as they hear parts composed by children now grown into young adulthood.

Reminiscent of the Jewish *shehecheyanu* prayer, Joan begins: "We thank You our maker for all the blessings that You have given us this year." Then she invites each person around the table to mention what they are thankful for. Afterwards, everyone joins together: "We thank You God for these and all things. Amen." Participants are asked to write down on small cards the items for which they are grateful. These cards are collected and added to the beginning blessing before each person adds something from the current year.

This attempt to find the right mix isn't about "choosing your battles." It is about understanding both the family and the religious contexts for family traditions, and establishing a supportive environment for a new family religious culture to be created out of various family traditions. It is also about respect and family comfort. Holidays needn't become "my" holiday or "his" holiday. The challenge of interfaith couples is to discover ways that make holidays "ours." Joan and Larry had established a Jewish home early in their marriage, so Jewish holidays are generally celebrated there. But they take their children to share the celebration of non-Jewish holidays in the homes of their relatives who observe them. The children, now in their late teen years and early twenties, understand that these choices were always about family, not religion. And they understand that their parents made these decisions with their children's best interests in mind. As a result, they recognize the importance of family and tradition more than many of their friends who are children of in-faith marriages.

THE DECEMBER DILEMMA

For many interfaith families, the similarities between Christmas and Hanukkah are more prominent than the differences. While the religious aspects are unrelated, they share similar roots in folk religion. For example, at the darkest time of the year, around the winter solstice, the natural tendency is to use light to push out the darkness. To ancient people, darkness represented sinister elements in the world, and they looked to religion to protect them against these elements. Light took a different meaning in emergent Christianity than it did in Rabbinic Judaism, even as it clung to some of its folk tradition. Jews use the light to symbolize the miracle of rededication of the Temple, commemorating the driving out of the Temple of the

Assyrian-Greeks and their idolatry. It also stands for the light of religious freedom. Ritually, candles are lit in special candelabras called menorahs or *hanukkiyot*. Christians use light as a symbol of the divine light that they believe Jesus brought into the world, and represent it with Christmas tree lights, some more elaborate than others. In both cases, the light is a symbol of the Divine.

As interfaith families come to identify with the Jewish community, the Christmas-Hanukkah dilemma may become more pronounced. Jewish holidays are essentially and practically different from Christian holidays, despite some similar sources. Christmas focuses on the birth of Jesus, whose role as Messiah is central to Christianity (and directly counter to Judaism, whose messianic vision remains unfulfilled). Hanukkah focuses on freedom from religious persecution and the attempt by traditionalists to keep Judaism intact, separate, and free from the influence of the dominant Hellenist culture. Hanukkah, then, can represent a contemporary desire to keep Judaism free from being overwhelmed by Christian culture. Hence the theological roots of the conflict between Hanukkah and Christmas.

In practice, conflicts sometimes emerge simply because of where the holidays fall on the calendar. When there are a few weeks between Hanukkah and Christmas, there is less competition. But in some years, a conflict suddenly emerges. Family members may be surprised, because they had no disagreements before.

Holidays can remind us of the loss of family left behind and thus renew yearnings for the past. When one casts her lot with a new religion and a new set of traditions, even without conversion, she may need to grieve the lost past. Acknowledging that loss is one way to show appreciation for the sacrifices your partner has made for the family you are creating.

This nostalgia or sense of "missing something" may lead your partner to seek out tokens of his past faith. One young husband, Paul, told me about being on vacation in Israel during the first year of marriage when he casually mentioned putting up a Christmas tree during the upcoming holiday. His wife, Ann, was alarmed; she thought everything had been decided. His reaction to her was "Wait a minute. Doesn't being married by a rabbi, having a huge Jerusalem print over the fireplace, and putting a *mezuzah* on almost every door in our new house buy me any credit in my own home?" By helping him to verbalize his pain and bewilderment, I was able to help his wife see his perspective. It probably also helped her to calm her relatives, whose reactions she had feared most in the first place. He was able to express his need to carve out a little space for his cherished Christmas symbol—and, by extension, his past—and she was able to accept it. In the end, he didn't put up the tree, but this mutual understanding has given their marriage a strong foundation.

After giving up on Christmas, and because she threw herself into preparing for her family's Jewish holidays, one non-Jewish mother told me, "I was actually relieved not to have to prepare for yet another holiday."

A close friend of mine, Sammy, described his experience with Christmas in a visceral way. He had been raised with the notion that not having a Christmas tree was in itself a Jewish act. As a child in Brooklyn, Sammy remembers coming home one day with a branch from a discarded tree. Without comment, his father opened up the window in their second-floor apartment and tossed the branch out, threatening to do the same with Sammy if he were ever to do "something like that" again. Years later, when Sammy married his second wife, Justine, he could intellectually understand her desire, as a practicing Christian, to set up a Christmas tree in their home, particularly for the benefit of the young daughter she had brought into the marriage. He even accompanied them to the Christmas tree lot to help them pick out the sturdiest and fullest tree. But when it came to putting it up in *his* home, he just couldn't do it. Sammy confided, "I felt violated, that I had betrayed my heritage and my past." While Sammy enthusiastically participated in Christmas celebrations at friends' homes, he just couldn't abide the thought of having a Christmas symbol in his own home. After Justine's conversion to Judaism, it was she who made the decision not to bring a Christmas tree into their home, so Sammy no longer had to struggle between his emotions (and the childhood memories at their source) and her desire to observe Christmas.

While we are not saying interfaith families should or shouldn't have Christmas trees in their homes, decisions about the details of such family traditions needn't reflect the religion in which you are raising your child. Sometimes a Christmas tree is just a generic American memory. On the other hand, Christian partners should understand that to Jews a Christmas tree is a ubiquitous symbol of Christian culture and is thus difficult to accept in their lives. As a result, the tree becomes a flashpoint for family resentment and anxiety. One young Jewish wife prepared her parents for the soon-to-arrive tree by saying, "I know this will be difficult for you. Just concentrate on the fact that although your friends' children won't have a Christmas tree in their homes, many of them won't have Jewish grandchildren. You do. Please don't make things difficult for me. I really need your help to make this work."

Find alternative ways to satisfy the desire to express the spirit of the season. Joan's parents instituted a yearly tree trimming/cooking/baking afternoon for all of their grandchildren. During years when the occasion fell during Hanukkah, Joan's daughters packed their menorahs in their suitcases to take with them to their grandparents' house. For Joan's children, these events became more of a cultural exchange than a religious event. Another good way to partake of Christmas without necessarily bringing it home is to volunteer in the community, serving meals and singing songs for those who lack the means to celebrate.

PASSOVER

More Jewish families celebrate Passover, in one form or another, than any other holiday. Perhaps this is because Passover is observed among family rather than in the synagogue; perhaps it is tangible proof of the timeliness of stories and the importance of memories. The Passover traditions in themselves provide a bridge to other cultures. The core lesson—that we must open our homes to the strangers in our midst because we were strangers in Egypt—serve as an entrée for welcoming the non-Jewish members of our family.

Moreover, while the Jewish community often overlooks it, the Passover saga's main character is in an interfaith marriage. After killing an Egyptian taskmaster whom he caught beating a Hebrew slave, Moses flees from Egypt to Midian. There he meets and falls in love with Zipporah, the daughter of a Midianite priest (read "local minister's daughter"). Her father, Jethro, becomes Moses' most important advisor. Perhaps our *sedarim* can be as welcoming of others as Jethro was of Moses.

Although there is no implicit theological conflict between Easter and Passover, there are many who believe that the Last Supper was, in fact, a Passover *seder*. Some families like to use it as a way for Christians to add experience and learning to their faith and even forge a link between Judaism and Christianity.

Furthermore, the Passover message of hope and optimism makes it perhaps the most significant Jewish holiday. I like to remind interfaith couples and their families of this message, particularly those who are struggling with challenges in their relationship.

HIGH HOLY DAYS

The High Holy Days of Rosh Hashanah and Yom Kippur, as well as the month of Elul that leads up to them, are times for self-reflection and repentance. As a result, they present interfaith couples and their families with the opportunity for understanding and the resolution of conflict. The process is woven into the emotional fabric of the holiday period. Use this time to consider your relationships with family members and to repair what may be broken. Unfortunately, some of the routines of our contemporary High Holy Days can interfere with the deeper messages.

Christian partners, for example, may be taken aback by the concept of synagogue dues or the need to buy holiday tickets, as opposed to the customary collection plate method of collecting funds in most churches. Decisions about whether to join and pay dues or buy tickets can be awkward for interfaith couples, who more than anything need a warm welcome. Then there are the messages from the pulpit about the ills of intermarriage, which seem to have become a High Holy Day perennial. It's best to find a synagogue that is sensitive to interfaith couples. They are out there.

The profound significance of the High Holy Days will have to be taught and modeled for your non-Jewish partner so that your partner's understanding will evolve over the years that you are together. Joan says, "Although the services often felt interminable, I have always loved having Larry whisper in my ear pertinent information and recall his childhood memories as the worship service progressed. Watching him instruct our children in that same intimate manner never fails to move me."

SHABBAT

The weekly Sabbath provides people with an opportunity to stand still amidst the shifting chaos of everyday life, to rest and be renewed. As a holiday, the Sabbath encapsulates many of the core values in Judaism. It provides us with a microcosm of a perfect world and our potential to realize one for ourselves. The Sabbath is liberating, because it forces us to let go of the daily work that still needs to get done—if only for one day. For interfaith families, the Sabbath may be a chance to free themselves temporarily from the conflicts in their lives, including those from their relationship. Begin with simple rituals, like eating *challah* and lighting candles—whatever you and your partner are most comfortable with. If you are not familiar with them, take the time to learn them together. Shabbat can grow as your family does. A teary-eyed friend of Joan recounted her Shabbat from the previous week. She had phoned home from the airport during an emergency trip out of town to find her children, aged two and five, preparing a Shabbat meal (complete with the appropriate blessings) with their Methodist father. It was clear to her that Jewish tradition didn't leave home when she did.

FESTIVALS FOCUSED ON CHILDREN

While the Jewish holidays were designed to be observed by the entire family, many North American synagogues have shaped their observances to be enjoyed primarily by children. This approach may not necessarily satisfy your religious needs or those of your partner, but it can immeasurably help the relationship with your parents and in-laws when you have children. Few grandparents are unmoved by their grandchildren's joyful holiday celebration. Adding children's holiday books to your family library and making time to read them can enrich their enjoyment. One family makes a visit to the bookstore as part of its holiday preparations. For days before the holiday, a collection of appropriate books sits in a basket in their family room to reflect the season.

Purim is a joyous festival, whose observation contains a great deal of frivolity. It has been relegated to a kind of "Jewish Halloween." The Purim story is read in the synagogue from a special scroll called a *megillah* (the origin of the phrase "the whole *megillah*"). Children and sometimes grown-ups dress up in costume and parade around the synagogue. Many communities have Purim carnivals on the Sunday preceding the holiday. There is very little ritual observance of the holiday; as a result, religious conflicts are minimal. Because it tends to be light and fun, it is a good point of entry for interfaith families. The custom of eating three-cornered pocket pastries (called hamantaschen, for the central villain in the story) is a delicious one. And what child can resist noisemakers?

Simchat Torah, which occurs at the end of the fall harvest festival of Sukkot, celebrates the conclusion of the annual cycle of the weekly Torah reading, as well as its beginning once again. While there are set rituals, Simchat Torah is a relatively chaotic, enthusiastic evening of parading and dancing with the Torah scrolls in the synagogue and, in some communities, outside in the street as well. Few ritual demands are placed on the individual, and little knowledge is required in order to enjoy it. Another fun, uncomplicated choice.

Tips

1. Remember that the goal of holiday celebrations is to bring families together and closer to the sacred, so be sure to make room for those elements in planning your observances.

2. Be careful to work with your partner. This includes being sensitive to your partner's emotional and spiritual needs, as well as seeing the observance of any holiday from his or her perspective. Remember to acknowledge your appreciation.

3. When you are deciding which holidays to celebrate and with whom, consider which holidays hold the most meaning for you and your partner, bring with them the least amount of conflict with your extended family, and will provide the most enduring memories for your children.

4. Look at holiday celebrations as steps on a journey through the sacred calendar of your life together. The addition of knowledge and experiences can help you to deepen the meaning of the journey.

6

LIFE-CYCLE EVENTS

Life-cycle events are those rituals and ceremonies that mark our journey through life from birth to death. Most religions have something to say and do during most such rites of passage. Jewish tradition also offers support for negative life-cycle events, like miscarriages and divorce. The rabbis that officiate at life-cycle ceremonies represent a variety of religious movements. Their affiliations govern a great deal of what they can and can't do.

Let's look at the four major movements. Reform rabbis operate under the same rules for personal autonomy as do Reform Jews, which gives them a good deal of discretion. The Central Conference of American Rabbis (the professional organization of Reform rabbis) offers guiding principles but, in general, leaves a great deal of flexibility. The Reconstructionist movement believes that the community has the right to make decisions that are incumbent on individual members of the community, including rabbis. However, since the movement is liberal, its rabbis tend to be liberal with regard to their officiation in life-cycle events. The Conservative movement is guided by what is called a Law Committee. Thus, its rabbis must follow the decisions of their professional association. Orthodox rabbis are required to follow solely a traditional interpretation of Jewish law. Thus, they too have little flexibility regarding their participation in life-cycle events involving Jews and non-Jews.

Similarly, each movement has its own standard regarding "who is a Jew." This basic assumption determines who may or may not participate in a life-cycle event or whether conversion is required. While the Reform and Reconstructionist movements accept as Jewish a child of a Jewish father who has been raised as a Jew—regardless of whether or not the mother is Jewish—Conservative and Orthodox Judaism only accept as Jewish the child of a Jewish mother.

It may seem as if the decisions that rabbis make are arbitrary and capricious. However, there are many caring and sensitive rabbis whose movements prohibit their participating in life-cycle events that involve non-Jews. Furthermore, even in the Reform and Reconstructionist movements, which permit such participation, rabbis are entitled to act according to their own conscience and beliefs. This may mean making decisions that appear to be exclusionary and unwelcoming.

INTRODUCTION: LOOKING BACK AT YOUR WEDDING

Let's start with the wedding. For those who decide to marry, this event initiates the transformation that launches them on their interfaith life together. Weddings leave us with profound and long-lasting memories—unfortunately, not all of them positive. The prospect of a wedding prompts many decisions that are complicated by interfaith relationships. They include where to hold the wedding, who will officiate, who can participate in the wedding party, whom to invite to the reception, and where to hold the reception.

As a result of tensions that arise from religious differences in planning the wedding, some couples carry animosity toward the Jewish community into the years that follow. Couples may come up against synagogues that prohibit interfaith weddings within their walls, and organizations whose newsletters refuse to report on the event. They may sense resistance from the rabbi. Rob and Mary, a couple I met as part of a discussion group, were angry at Rob's rabbi. Rob had grown up with this man and at one time had felt very attached to him. Yet, when it was time for him to officiate at Rob's wedding to Mary, the rabbi was totally unsupportive. It is important to wrestle with these unpleasant feelings early on and resolve them so that they don't cast a shadow over the first few years of your marriage.

Many synagogue-based discussion groups designed to support intermarried couples begin by addressing wedding-related resentments that still linger. Couples may need to air their grievances before they are able to move forward with their marriage and their relationship to the Jewish community. Sometimes it just takes an acknowledgment of a couple's pain for them to be able to let go of it and move forward with their lives. In one group, almost immediately after I reminded Rob and Mary that, upsetting as events might have been, their wedding ceremony was all of fifteen minutes long—and five years ago at that—they realized that it was time to put it behind them and focus on the good they had now.

The choices you make at the outset and how you make them set the stage for life-cycle events yet to come. Take into account your own feelings and your family's feelings, as well as the perspective of the clergy with whom you are working. Consider also the attitudes of the community you hope to join. Focus on your needs as a couple, rather than as two individuals. This takes practice. In the discussion that follows, we offer background on individual life-cycle events and what you may expect during these rituals, and guidance on interfaith issues that may emerge.

BABY NAMINGS AND CIRCUMCISIONS

In chapter 4, we urged you to think ahead about the general questions of how you will raise your children. It's also best to think ahead, before the children are born, about specific rituals that welcome them as well. One interfaith couple called me recently from the hospital room, the pregnant mother now confined to her bed.

They had yet to make a decision about *brit milah* (ritual circumcision ceremony), and they were only a week away from the due date—yet they had known it was to be a boy for months! They were already nervous about the impending birth, having tried for years to get pregnant. As I informed them of the available options, I wished that they had spoken to me much earlier in the pregnancy. They would have had the luxury of time in which to make the decision that would be right for them. They could have spoken with others who had found themselves in similar circumstances. It is difficult for anyone to carefully consider such important decisions under the pressure of time and the emotional stress of such an impending event in their lives.

Many people offer all kinds of information about the Jewish "rules" surrounding birth, but much of it is hearsay. The Jewish religion has some ritual requirements, like the *brit milah*. Beyond that, however, customs surrounding the *brit milah* and naming are optional. Don't let the fact that you are an interfaith couple deter you from making certain choices.

The flexibility in the Jewish tradition allows for creativity in the naming ceremony, as well as in the participation of family members and friends who are not Jewish. However, as an interfaith family you might discuss with the officiant, as early as is reasonable, such issues as who may participate in the ceremony and the specific content of the ceremony. Many, but by no means all, couples know the sex of the baby in advance. Still, there's a fifty-fifty chance you will have a boy and thus be having a *brit milah*. Knowing this, take the opportunity to review the options and communicate to family and friends at leisure and not under stress.

As your experience in preparation for a wedding probably taught you, some officiants are more flexible than others with regard to the participation of non-Jews in the ceremony. This may be determined by the officiant's ideological viewpoint as much as by Jewish law. Take the time to find someone whose views are compatible with yours. This may not be easy. If the mother of the child is Jewish, fewer issues about who will officiate may arise, since the child will be regarded as Jewish by all denominations. If the mother is not Jewish, you will be more limited in who can officiate, since the child will be recognized as Jewish only by the Reform and Reconstructionist movements. Thus, make your plans early.

In most cases, you can personalize the ceremony. This is particularly helpful for interfaith couples who want to acknowledge both sides of the family regardless of religion. Traditional Jewish ceremonies welcome children to life as well as to the community. While there are no "rules" on readings, you may want to review the choices you have made with the officiant. You may want to consider having the ceremony take place at home in order to avoid any restrictive policies and procedures in a given synagogue.

In Jewish tradition, boys are generally named during a *brit milah* ceremony performed by a *mohel* (a trained ritual circumciser). Most *mohalim* (plural of *mohel*) will perform the ceremony only if the child's mother is Jewish or if there is a clear intention to convert the child (initiated through the *brit milah* and immersion in a ritual bath). Others are willing to do so if the baby's father is Jewish and the parents have decided to raise the child Jewishly, and specifically not "in two faiths." Since a boy is supposed to be circumcised on his eighth day of life, you don't have much time to make arrangements. Again, this is why it is important to make some plans before the birth, even if you don't know the child's sex.

Consult the resources in the back of this book for help in locating a local interfaith-friendly *mohel*. Detailed descriptions of the ceremony and options for interfaith families are available in Anita Diamant's *New Jewish Baby Book: Names, Ceremonies and Customs—A Guide for Today's Families* (Jewish Lights Publishing). Invite caring friends to help newcomers—especially non-Jews new to the family—through the ritual. It is important to invite non-Jewish friends and family members who will be part of your child's life so that they can become acquainted with his Jewish home and its practices. The rituals will also provide you with an excellent opportunity to educate your new relatives about Judaism and Jewish life.

It used to be common for a girl to be named quickly and

perfunctorily during the reading of the Torah in the synagogue on the first Sabbath morning after her birth. Among liberal Jewish synagogues, there has been a concerted effort to give parents a ritual opportunity similar to the *brit milah* to celebrate the birth of a daughter. While there is still no time limit on the naming ceremony for girls, we encourage parents to do so very early in a child's life. Because there is no formal tradition in the naming of girls, you will have even more latitude for the personalization of the ceremony and the involvement of whomever you choose. Choose a name that is meaningful to you and your partner. For assistance, consult Debra Nussbaum Cohen, *Celebrating Your New Jewish Daughter: Creating Jewish Ways to Welcome Baby Girls into the Covenant—New and Traditional Ceremonies* (Jewish Lights Publishing).

BAR AND BAT MITZVAH

The bar or bat mitzvah is a rite of passage that marks the transition from childhood into adulthood. Whether the transition is marked by a ceremony and celebration or not, girls come of age at twelve and boys at thirteen according to Jewish law. For those who convert their children to Judaism as infants, this age is extremely important. Jewish law requires that converts affirm their conversion (their Jewish choice) at adulthood—that is, at age twelve or thirteen. The bar or bat mitzvah, as a public act of affirmation, satisfies this requirement. (In an effort to promote equality among the sexes, most liberal synagogues no longer make the distinction between girls and boys and the respective ages but make it thirteen for both.) In some cases, rabbis may use the bar or bat mitzvah as a conversion ritual for children whose parents did not formally convert them to Judaism. In the case of the Reform and Reconstructionist movements, which accept patrilineal descent for the religious status of a child, the bar and bat mitzvah serve as a way of affirming the presumption of Jewish identity that is required by these movements. If you consider this approach, note that other movements will not accept this act of affirmation—and neither will some family members.

Since bar and bat mitzvah ceremonies are generally not private affairs, they should reflect the policies set by the congregation in which they are celebrated. This is where interfaith families usually face numerous challenges: determining what is considered and not considered permissible. It is usually the ritual committee of a synagogue that sets forth the policies that decide who can participate in a bar or bat mitzvah and what they can do, but some synagogues are reluctant to print such regulations. Instead, they leave it to the rabbi to represent those policies to interfaith families. In some synagogues, ritual committees leave pulpit-related issues completely to the discretion of the rabbi. Thus, he or she may determine who may be invited to stand on the pulpit, and what honor (as most of the Torah-related activities are called) may be given to the participants. These honors include opening the holy ark so that the Torah scrolls can be removed or returned, saying the blessings before and after the Torah reading, carrying the Torah, raising the Torah, and dressing the Torah.

Knowing this should help you plan. What role may a non-Jewish parent have in the ceremony? Can she be called to the Torah with the Jewish parent if the Jewish parent recites the blessing before and after the Torah reading? Can a non-Jewish parent address the child in a parent's message to the bar or bat mitzvah? Can she recite the traditional parent's prayer? In congregations where the Torah is handed down from one generation to the next (what is referred to as the Torah transmission ceremony), can a non-Jewish parent participate and actually handle the Torah? Can a non-Jewish parent even stand on the *bimah* (the raised platform in the front of the synagogue)? Don't make assumptions about what is permitted. Be specific with your questions.

Since there may be a large number of non-Jewish relatives who may not be familiar with the particular synagogue's customs, you may want to include a separate note about various "dos and don'ts" along with the invitation. Some families prepare small booklets that guide guests through the prayer liturgy and the ceremony itself, as well as general Sabbath policies at the synagogue. People always feel more comfortable when they know more about what to expect and what is expected of them. Children spend a great deal of time preparing for their bar or bat mitzvah, and it is a shame when family faux pas threaten to eclipse these accomplishments, especially when they could have been avoided. Consult Jeffrey Salkin's *Putting God on the Guest List: How to Reclaim the Spiritual Meaning of Your Child's Bar or Bat Mitzvah* and *For Kids—Putting God on Your Guest List: How to Claim the Spiritual Meaning of Your Bar or Bat Mitzvah* (both Jewish Lights Publishing) for basic information about the ceremony, service, and suggestions for a more spiritually meaningful event. (In *Putting God on the Guest List,* see the special appendix, which you can photocopy and distribute to members of your family and friends.)

Don't wait until the last minute to work out family details. The bar or bat mitzvah can be a powerful spiritual experience in the life of a child and his or her family. It can be pivotal in affirming a child's identity. The event also presents you with an opportunity to cement bonds with the members of your extended family, including those new to Jewish ritual.

WEDDINGS ONCE AGAIN

Your wedding marked the beginning of your transition from an interfaith couple to an interfaith family. Your choice to become an interfaith couple also affects the marriage of your children years later, when they approach clergy about their own marriage. They may face Jewish status questions for the first time. If an adult child's mother was not born into Judaism, some rabbis will require proof either that she converted or that the child did—and that the conversion was affirmed in adulthood, as discussed previously in this chapter. Since rabbis from the various movements in Judaism have different perspectives on the question of Jewish status, the extent to which your child feels questioned (or interrogated) may depend on the rabbi's affiliation. Saying "I am Jewish" may not be sufficient and may require corroboration by another rabbi or by some documentation. Some rabbis may even require a conversion before the wedding, even for children who have been raised as Jews but who may not be considered technically Jewish according to traditional Jewish law. One young man confided in me that he was embarrassed to tell his fiancee's family that he had to formally convert before the wedding. He had always considered himself Jewish, and he was angry that his parents had not considered this issue early in his life and dealt with it. News about status may come as a surprise to your children. As a result, unresolved anger about your own choices that have affected them may surface with the added emotional stress of preparation.

FUNERALS

Questions about the death of one partner in an interfaith couple are usually straightforward. Will a rabbi officiate at the funeral of a non-Jewish spouse? And can a non-Jewish spouse be buried in a Jewish cemetery?

I recall a quite prominent Jewish family who were members of a large synagogue in town. The children were Jewishly well educated, and the mother participated in all aspects of Jewish life. However, out of respect for her own parents, she had never formally converted to Judaism. Her husband died and was buried in a Jewish cemetery. At age ninety, her own parents now long gone, she felt there was no point in converting. But she had lived a Jewish life since her marriage nearly seventy years earlier and wanted to die as a Jew. She wanted to be buried among the people with whom she had lived. She thought that buying a plot next to her husband would be simple. But the local Reform congregation debated for months before coming to the resolution that it was willing to accept her in death as it had in life—though not before some members resigned from the congregation as a result of the tense discussions concerning the decision.

Synagogue and cemetery burial policies vary, as do rabbinic attitudes toward officiating at the funeral of non-Jews. However, more rabbis will officiate at the funerals of non-Jewish spouses than would have at the same couples' weddings. Such rabbis say, "It's unclear what the spouses will do at marriage, but at death we can see what the person actually demonstrated in a lifetime."

Some people think they can avoid problems by choosing non-sectarian cemeteries. However, some rabbis can't officiate in cemeteries that are not Jewish, particularly if any Christian symbols are present in the cemetery.

Some rabbis and cemetery officials may believe that according to Jewish law it is not permissible to bury non-Jews in Jewish cemeteries. This is, however, not clear. For example, Rabbi Solomon Freehof (1892–1990) argued that only the actual burial place of the Jew is sanctified as Jewish ground. As a result, he made the point that technically there is no such thing as a Jewish cemetery, only Jewish graves. Others formally demarcate non-Jewish graves, such as with railings, but still find ways to include them within the larger communal area of the Jewish cemetery. Therefore, any argument against burying non-Jews in a Jewish cemetery on "legal" grounds should not close the door to further discussion.

Rabbi Michael Hertzbrun, a congregational rabbi in upstate New York, tells this story about the way creative thinking about interfaith burials can have a profound impact on the religious lives of entire families:

A couple from my former congregation tracked me down in my new community and asked me to officiate at their wedding. During the reception, a young man approached me and said, "Rabbi, it is wonderful to see you again. It is because of you that I am still a Jew." I was somewhat taken aback, as I did not recognize him and had no clue as to what he was talking about. "Forgive me, but I don't know who you are," I replied. He responded, "I am Pearl's grandson." I hugged him, and both of us began to cry. It had been ten years since I had been called back to that same congregation, not for a wedding but for a funeral. It was his grandmother who died, and while she had been active in the life of the synagogue and its sisterhood for over forty years, no one realized that she had never formally converted to Judaism. The local Orthodox synagogue that owned the cemetery would not allow her to be buried there. The family called me and asked if I would do her funeral. I said that I would, and further suggested that they buy a multigrave section of the local secular cemetery, and mark the area off with pebbles. They did so, and before burying the young man's grandmother, I consecrated the area as a Jewish cemetery.

Most cemetery policies are a matter of synagogue record, so ask for a copy of them. But remember that policies change. It's also possible to discuss the rules with synagogue leaders, particularly since these rules are generally reviewed only when challenged. Sometimes raising questions about burial policies for interfaith families will encourage committees to review other ritual policies as well, especially when individual family members have demonstrated congregational participation and leadership.

Tips

1. Each Jewish religious movement has its own standards. Similarly, each community and synagogue that adheres to a particular movement has its own guidelines. Before making any decisions about life-cycle events, find out about policies by asking its leadership or office staff rather than making assumptions or listening to those who think they know. Policies regularly change, so keep yourself up to date.

2. Prepare family members for what to expect in a given ceremony. You may want to prepare a booklet of explanations for family unfamiliar with the traditions.

3. Before planning which family members to include, make sure that both the community and the persons involved are comfortable with your plans for the ceremony itself.

7

NURTURING THE JEWISH SPIRIT AND SOUL

While previous chapters in this book have explored your role as the Jewish partner in an interfaith relationship in helping to establish and nurture a Jewish home, this chapter focuses on maintaining your Jewish self. How you sustain your own Jewish identity and spiritual needs is not necessarily contingent on the decisions that your partner has made about Judaism or on the decisions that you both have made regarding your children, but it may be more difficult within an interfaith relationship. On the other hand, your non-Jewish partner may be pivotal in renewing your Judaism or helping to raise it to a higher level. This is frequently the case in interfaith relationships. Thus, this chapter will also identify ways in which your non-Jewish partner can help support your Jewish identity and thereby help you to care for the Jewish identity of your family. We will consider some essential questions regarding Jewish spirituality in the context of an interfaith relationship, while also exploring its practical implications in your community and home.

How to Nurture Your Own Soul: Ritual, Study, Prayer

At this point in your relationship, you may feel reluctant to maintain a Jewish life. Perhaps your feelings result from your own apathy toward Judaism, or perhaps you feel uneasy about actively pursuing your Jewish identity while in an interfaith relationship. You may think it unfair to impose Judaism or any aspect of it on your non-Jewish partner. Perhaps you just don't know much "Jewish stuff" or think that Judaism is only what you left behind when you finished Sunday school as an adolescent. Your hesitancy may come from feeling Jewishly illiterate, rather than from actual disinterest in Judaism or religion in general. There may be more in Judaism than you think. While you might have some sense of what Jewish religious tradition has to offer you as an adult, it is important to discover the elements in it for your life as a partner in an interfaith relationship.

On the other hand, if you *are* a practicing Jew, your making a commitment to someone not Jewish does not mean you have to closet away personal rituals and religious traditions that might have previously marked your life. Your partner will probably want to learn about these rituals, particularly if they are an important part of your life, even if he or she is not ready to adopt them. It is also quite possible that some of these traditions may assume new significance in your life and Jewish identity now that you are involved in an interfaith relationship.

Given the community-oriented nature of Judaism, it is difficult to nurture it in isolation. This is even more so in an interfaith relationship, when another religion is pulling on you like an undertow. Consider joining a synagogue, study group, or Jewish Community Center (JCC). The relationships you form by tapping into a Jewish community will help you develop and sustain a personal routine of spiritual development.

Three basic elements are indispensable to developing and maintaining a spiritual life in Judaism: ritual, study, and prayer. Each complements the others. Jewish tradition has determined fixed

times for each while simultaneously making room for their sponta-
neous expression. Traditionally, Jews engage in many ritual practices
that help guide their daily life (providing opportunities to say one
hundred blessings each day for everything from waking up to finishing a meal), study regularly, and pray three times a day (morning,
midday, and evening). Some people find it easier simply to follow
patterns already established by Jewish tradition. Others prefer to
develop their own pattern of spiritual practices and thereby create a
unique personal religious rhythm for themselves, often combining
innovation with tradition. These may include setting aside time to
meditate in the morning as a complement or substitute for the prescribed traditional morning ritual of prayers. The traditional models
for spiritual practice can serve as a guide or a goal to strive toward.
A community can help you find guidance, support, and the right
place to start.

Your partner may feel uncomfortable about your decision to
join a community. That's why it is important to make your intention
known as early in your relationship as possible. And encourage your
partner to participate in the community from the outset. He or she
may not feel welcome—or even know that participation is
allowed—unless you make your invitation explicit. In some communities this may be difficult, because they may not be as welcoming and inclusive as we might like. In some communities it will be
easy because they see it as their responsibility to make your partner
feel welcome, not just welcome the partner officially. But participating together can potentially bring you closer together, while participating alone may have the unintended effect of driving you apart.
The sharing of meaningful spiritual experiences is important in
building and solidifying a long-term relationship.

Ritual

We all ritualize our lives. We have routines that we follow each day,
from the moment we wake up in the morning until we go to bed at
night. The challenge in living a spiritual life is how to raise the

mundane routine to the sacred, to the holy. Jewish rituals help us do so. They assist us in making concrete the abstract ideas in Judaism. They bring us closer to God and, in so doing, closer to ourselves.

Bringing Jewish rituals into your life can provide an anchor amidst the chaos of the everyday. They can help you bridge the gap that is often felt between the secular and the sacred, between you and the Divine. Effective rituals are those that enhance the closeness you are trying to develop.

Historically, living a ritual life has required a great deal of discipline, personal commitment, and religious literacy. As a result, people often opted out, particularly those who felt in command of many aspects of their lives and professions but felt ignorant about Jewish ritual. Many who intermarried felt that they had abandoned Judaism, if only because that is what the community told them. What many people don't realize is that you can enter Jewish ritual life anywhere along its continuum, at any pace that feels comfortable for you. Don't let others' views restrict you. Let your heart guide you instead. Stay with a practice or even a small part of a practice until you own it, until you feel comfortable with it.

A good place to start is with blessings said at meals. (Guidance is available from the resources listed at the end of the book.) These table blessings are simple rituals that don't require any ritual objects. They can be said individually or can be grouped together to form a meal routine. You can say them by yourself or with a group of people. And everyone has to eat. The practice of saying table blessings can simply be added to your snacks and meals, rather than requiring an entirely separate routine that is not part of your usual daily life. Non-Jewish partners may bring the practice of table blessings with them from their own religious tradition. Thus, the experience may not be new to them, only the specific vocabulary and approach. Invite them to join in this ritual as long they are comfortable in doing so.

You can move on to other ritual practices—when you choose to do so. And your partner can join you, as well. There is no required set path in ritual life. The important thing is not *where* you begin or *how* you begin; the important thing is *that* you begin.

Study

Study regularly. You may want to begin on Shabbat afternoon as a way of marking the Sabbath as a day different from the rest. The regular study of sacred texts keeps us centered and focused. Thus, we should do as much study of sacred text as possible. For when we study, says the tradition, the presence of God dwells among us. Just reading and thinking about the prayer book or Torah translation is a sufficient place to begin. The Torah is a dynamic document. It becomes real when we enter into it and, in so doing, become one with our ancestors, living and struggling among them. And when we conclude our study, the legacy of our ancestors remains in our soul, and we have left a little of ourselves in the text.

Rabbi Norman J. Cohen, author of *The Way Into Torah,* says that we should imbibe the power and flavor of every aspect of the Torah text, attending closely to all its details and allowing ourselves to be touched by it. Every word, every symbol, every phrase is ripe with meaning. Only upon engaging in Torah will we begin to see our spiritual journeys reflected in it and gain a greater sense of who we are and where we are going. By living with the text, we can reach the point where the Torah begins to reverberate within our souls. By bringing ourselves to the sacred stories of Torah, we gain insight into our own natures and our own search for meaning.

Try beginning your study with the traditional blessing of study: *Barukh ata Adonai, Elohenu Melekh ha-olam asher kidshanu b'mitzvotav vitzivanu la'asok bidivrei Torah.* Praised are You, Adonai our God, Sovereign of the universe, who makes us holy with *mitzvot* (sacred obligations) and instructs us to busy ourselves with the words and works of Torah. This blessing helps us distinguish sacred study from everyday activity. Jewish tradition has offered us this formula, which opens up a dialogue with the Divine and provides us with a sacred context for learning.

Raising Jewish children begins with a committed and educated parent. In your interfaith relationship, you will probably assume responsibility for your children's Jewish education. You can't leave it to your spouse or even to a Jewish school. Unfortunately, this often does not happen when the Jewish parent is the father, since men still tend to leave primary parenting responsibilities—including religious education—to their spouses. Therefore, as an adult you will have to learn a great deal more about Judaism in a shorter time than you may have anticipated. As one intermarried friend put it, "When we married, I realized that it was going to be my responsibility to raise our Jewish kids. As a man, I hadn't even considered that. And I was scared 'cause I didn't really know that much. Raising Jewish children challenged my manhood and my Jewish identity. But it also affirmed both as I studied regularly, and my wife studied along with me. Then together we taught our children."

Prayer

However you begin, I believe that developing a personal relationship with the Divine is pivotal in establishing a spiritual life and the nurturing of your Jewish soul. After all, the goal of Jewish spirituality is to develop a relationship with God, as originally expressed in the covenant between God and the Jewish people established at Sinai. If you begin your self-nurturing with prayer, you may either want to start with traditional formulas for prayer or use the words that emerge directly from your heart.

Start simply. Take for example, the *shema,* and use it as a *kavannah,* or sacred mantra, in the morning and in the evening. Reflect on it. Meditate on it. Try to recite it at the same times of day, just after rising and just before retiring for the night. Then, one at a time, surround it with other prayers. Follow this practice with other prayers, such as the core Jewish prayer, the *amidah,* around which our three daily services are constructed. Rabbi Ed Feinstein, of Valley Beth Shalom in Encino, California, tells us that the Hasidim have a tradition that each word of the *amidah* prayer is deserving of its own intense concentration. He advises us to say each word and stay there until we have internalized the word fully. It is the only way, he says, that we can fully realize the power of each word for our lives. While it may be unrealistic to focus on each word in the entire prayer (since that would take about three hours just for this prayer alone), choose a few words each day to focus on. It may take some time, but you may experience the potential for transformation.

CULTURAL SPIRITUALITY

For me, creating a Jewish spiritual life includes making a place for God in our lives. However, I recognize that many Jews are open to different avenues of spiritual fulfillment. Some of these involve acts of social justice or support for the State of Israel. They may volunteer at local soup kitchens or rally for Israel or raise funds on Israel's behalf. Some study sacred texts for intellectual stimulation rather than to cultivate a connection with the Divine. They study Jewish history and philosophy and read Jewish novels. Some attend classes regularly or belong to a study group that meets regularly. Some find spiritual fulfillment in Jewish art and music and film. They may volunteer as a docent at a local Jewish museum or become regular participants in Jewish film festivals and concerts. Still others take on traditional ritual practice to create a spiritual anchor in their lives that may have nothing to do with their relationship with God. Rather, they see the simple beauty inherent in certain rituals or their transcendent ability to bind families together in meaningful experiences. We affirm them all.

YOUR PARTNER'S SPIRITUAL LIFE

Your new or renewed interest in Jewish life may initially be unsettling for your non-Jewish partner. Your partner might have anticipated a secular home life with merely a modicum of Jewish culture. This may in fact be a significant change for a partner who did not experience Jewish—or perhaps any religious—culture during childhood. The establishment of a Jewish home may seem like a daunting task. Thus, encourage your spouse to be an *equal* partner in your spiritual life. Non-Jewish partners often find themselves spiritually nourished and enriched as a result. Invite your partner to explore his or her own religious heritage. Don't downplay your partner's sense of spirituality or expect that he or she can put aside years of spiritual learning and growth. Your partner's religious past and the parents who helped form it are part of the person he or she has become.

Interfaith families often focus on the tension that emerges between what they perceive as two conflicting religious cultures. Admittedly, tension consumes a great deal of energy in interfaith families. But by focusing on the conflict, you may run the risk of missing the opportunity to see where your religious backgrounds can complement each other. This is the area of faith in God. Belief in God can be a core value in a family's life, irrespective of the particular religious backgrounds of couples. This is what Rabbi Tirzah Firestone, who led the Jewish Renewal Congregation in Boulder, Colorado, likes to call "the third way."

For example, Joan was always a religious woman. Through all these years in an interfaith marriage, Joan has always believed that God is the key factor in the decisions she has made for herself and for her children. Yet, she also realizes that God is a minor factor for most "intermarriage worriers." They worry about holidays and family relations and synagogue politics. She says, "Perhaps if they worried more about the role God plays in their lives—and in the decisions that they make—everything would work out better." Joan attributes her successful interfaith marriage to many factors, but above all to her own reliance on and faith in God, for whom she has always made room in her life and the life of her family.

There are those intermarried partners for whom belief in God is not central to their lives, but will want to support you in your belief. What is most important is that together you find a way for your partner's belief to complement your own.

YOUR FAMILY'S SPIRITUAL LIFE

Each family's spiritual rhythm is different. This rhythm changes over time, often accelerating during holiday seasons and in anticipation of the life-changing events such as the birth of a child. Even if there are profound differences in your family's approach to religion, let the similarities in your spiritual yearnings bind you together.

THE JEWISH COMMUNITY: FINDING A WELCOMING PLACE

Some synagogues still struggle with establishing relationships with interfaith families. They don't understand how an interfaith family can support the Jewish partner's religious identity. Others, like Congregation Sukkat Shalom in Wilmette, Illinois (in suburban Chicago), under the leadership of Rabbi Sam Gordon, find it no struggle at all. Theirs is a truly egalitarian synagogue. All members are equal, regardless of their religious backgrounds. All members participate fully. All are encouraged to take active roles in the synagogue and its ritual. In many cases, it is the non-Jew who teaches the Jew—and the entire community learns as a result. And the outcome is a culturally diverse institution that is very Jewish at its core.

You can tell rather quickly whether a community is right for you and your family. When Joan asked Rabbi Arnie Sleutelberg of Congregation Shir Tikvah in Troy, Michigan, about the number of interfaith families in his congregation, he cautioned, "I don't count them. If I did, it would mean that we care about numbers. We don't care about numbers. We care about people."

Nevertheless, keep in mind that opportunities to connect to the Jewish community transcend the walls of the synagogue. As you venture into the community, there will undoubtedly be some institutions that will not welcome you as a partner in an interfaith relationship. This attitude is not limited to synagogues or to those who want to work professionally in the Jewish community. Some institutions will not even welcome your volunteer leadership, fearing that you are not an appropriate model for the community. There is a place in the Jewish community for everyone. But because it can be challenging to find, it is all the more important to assume the personal obligation for nurturing your own soul.

ESSENTIAL SPIRITUALITY

For many, spirituality has little to do with formal religion at all. This neutral aspect of spirituality can serve as a template for your new family. While many people define spirituality in terms of feelings, I like to say that spirituality is about bringing people closer to the Divine. And that is pretty important—and profoundly deeper than emotions, which come and go. Nevertheless, feelings help pave the path for a connection with the Divine. When you get close to God, you may in fact feel pretty good. It is indeed an awesome experience.

While the Jewish community is doing a better job of speaking about God and spirituality than in the past, non-Jewish partners are often more practiced at it and more comfortable in doing so. Thus, your non-Jewish partner might have much to teach you about spirituality. Though you may talk about the most intimate things with your partner, it may take some time for you to be able to talk about God. But the proximity to the Divine and the desire to seek it can provide a common spiritual element for you both, even as you figure out the role of Judaism in your own lives. In fact, this common spiritual element can help get you there. Reflecting on the early years of her marriage, Joan felt that in order to participate in establishing a Jewish home, she needed to feel that her personal spiritual needs were respected and honored. She might have agreed to remove the visual signs of her Christian spirituality, but her religious practice—prayer, relating to the sacred and the holy, feeling God's presence—was still there and needed sustenance. Judaism helped to give expression to those desires, which never left.

Spirituality is more discussed among Jews than perhaps ever before. While once considered to be on the periphery of Jewish life, spirituality has come to the center. Some might say that it has reshaped the center. Today's spirituality, however, is not necessarily expressed according to classic Jewish practice. It may be surprising to your non-Jewish partner, particularly if he or she was raised in an actively practicing religious family, to find that the overt concepts of faith, God, prayer, and belief may be seen as side issues to many Jews and to their identity as Jewish people.

THE PRACTICAL IMPLICATIONS OF SPIRITUALITY: ESTABLISHING A JEWISH HOME

Before determining how to establish a Jewish home, we need to ask what makes a Jewish home. It is easy to list the things that should be included, provided that the ritual objects on the list are there to be used and not simply displayed as artifacts. In addition to ritual objects for Sabbath and holidays, we could add Jewish art that shapes the cultural ambience of the home and Jewish books and magazines and newspapers that have an impact on the intellectual life of the family. However, what most marks a Jewish home are the values of those who live in it. These values are often described in cultural terms that have been suggested by the ancient Rabbis, but what they hold in common is that they are based on a relationship between God and each person and, consequently, between people.

That's why the first indicator of a Jewish home is a *mezuzah* on the front door frame, and sometimes on every door frame in the house (except the one to the bathroom). The *mezuzah* contains the *shema* blessing and its supporting texts from the Bible. For some, this will simply identify your home as a Jewish home. That may be enough. But on a deeper level these words on the *mezuzah's* scrolls remind us that this house is one in which God's presence is acknowledged, and God's direction for our lives is heeded.

Tips

1. Make room in your life for a spirituality that includes the routine of daily prayer, frequent study of sacred literature, and regular ritual observance.

2. Support your spouse in translating spiritual yearnings into Jewish terms.

3. Be proactive about Jewish spirituality in your family life and in your home. Be a model for your spouse and children to follow.

4. Join a synagogue or other Jewish communal group that will support your efforts to study, pray, and practice Jewish ritual. Make sure to choose one that will actively welcome your non-Jewish partner.

8

Marrying Later in Life

We have devoted most of this book to issues that arise in interfaith relationships among younger people. However, people today are getting married later in life. Many such couples are having fewer or no children, or together are bringing up children from previous marriages. Some couples decide not to marry but live together in a committed relationship. This is particularly true among older adults. Second marriages are more likely to be interfaith than first marriages. Interfaith issues may be no less challenging for more mature couples than for younger ones, but the challenges may be somewhat different.

Often, in the case of second marriages, the first partner was Jewish. When the new partner isn't Jewish, the children may be as critical as parents might be for younger couples. If these children are now adults, they may be outspoken about a parent's choice as if it were a betrayal of their religious beliefs. However, since they are no longer living at home and their religious identities have already been shaped, they will probably exert less impact on any decisions. If you are older, your relationship to your parents (if they are still living) and the responsibility you feel toward them in your decision about your new life partner will probably be less problematic.

However, adding multiple religious traditions to years of accumulated past relationships and experiences significantly increases the possibilities of interpersonal and family clashes. When problems occur, it is not unusual for partners to blame these problems on the difference between religions. In the midst of a counseling session, Kathy told me that she was shaken to the core when Sammy said to her, "If only I had married Rachel, I would not have these problems." She knew what "Rachel" meant. Rachel was the Jewish woman Sam had dated all through college. That is why it is important to evaluate each situation on its own merit and anticipate conflicts related to religious differences that may arise.

THOSE MARRYING FOR THE FIRST TIME

If you have never been married and are now marrying later in life, you may face fewer social challenges to your interfaith relationship. As you no doubt know yourself better, you may also be better able to withstand pressure from the family and the Jewish community than someone younger. Your openness to marrying someone who isn't Jewish may stem from a previous interfaith relationship that foundered because of religious differences. Perhaps you regret that decision. Maybe you don't want to make the same "mistake" again. Families often seem to be so happy when a grown child has finally "found someone" that religious issues previously considered insurmountable are now taken in stride.

One woman, herself a widow after nearly sixty years of marriage, confided to me recently that her fifty-year-old daughter, Samantha, had never been married and was now dating Phil, a non-Jewish man. Samantha was hesitant about marrying him, since maintaining her Jewish identity was very important to her. She had long given up on having children, and his children were already grown. Samantha's mother told her, "You have to decide what is more important to you right now: continuing to be alone or marrying a Jewish man." Perhaps without even realizing it, Samantha had been waiting for her mother to give her permission to marry Phil.

Parents are not always so supportive or understanding. Their attitudes continue to confound their children, no matter their age. Meredith, who is in her forties, told me that her parents were extremely welcoming of her non-Jewish boyfriend from the first time she introduced him to them. They said nothing about his Christian practices, since they were so delighted that she had finally "found someone." Meredith had gone to an afternoon Hebrew school when she was a child, but her parents discontinued their synagogue membership after her bat mitzvah. That was about thirty years ago. But once Meredith announced her engagement, they began talking about how important it was that her fiance convert to Judaism before they could be married—in a synagogue and by a rabbi, of course!

PREVIOUSLY MARRIED TO A JEW

If your first partner was Jewish, you may want to recreate the type of Jewish home and routine that you once had—even though that marriage ultimately failed. On the other hand, you may recognize that marrying a Jewish person is no guarantee of a successful marriage. Therefore, you feel that it is more important to find someone to be a life companion to complement who you are, regardless of his or her religious preference or practice. Don't expect to be able to create the same religious life you had with your first partner. Use the opportunity of a new partnership to create a life that reflects the current stage of your spiritual and religious journey.

PREVIOUSLY MARRIED TO A NON-JEW

If your first partner was not Jewish, you may feel that it is easier to marry a non-Jew a second time. On the other hand, you may be fearful that religious or cultural differences will doom this marriage as well. Sharon came to see me for advice when her second marriage was in trouble. After her first marriage, her Jewish family remained cordial, but she was not as close to them as she had once been. That made her second marriage to a non-Jew rather easy. By that time, she really didn't much care what her family felt, since she was so distant from them. However, she admitted to me her fear that the same issues of religious conflict that ultimately ruined her first marriage could potentially destroy her second marriage too. It took some time for her to realize that it was both her former husband's and her lack of flexibility that had made it so difficult to iron out religious disagreements. And both her first and second husbands shared the character trait of being stubborn! Such a personality can play havoc in an interfaith marriage.

AFTER A DEATH

Losing a spouse to death, whether sudden or after a prolonged period of illness, is markedly different from losing a partner through divorce. Both require some sort of mourning period. Yet, community support during bereavement after the death of a spouse is built into the Jewish practice. There is no prescribed requirement of time before a person can remarry. Yet, we recommend that if you are widowed, you should wait a reasonable period of time before entering a new relationship, particularly an interfaith relationship. You need to be sure that the pain of your loss does not obscure your ability to think clearly through the issues that you will have to confront in an interfaith relationship. Just because your first marriage was a good one does not mean that a second relationship will be so. In addition, others in your family, particularly children, may require time to heal before they are able to support your decision to remarry.

DIVORCE

We want to preserve family relationships. Therefore, if we understand some of the fault lines in interfaith marriages that may lead to divorce, we may be able to offer possible solutions. Research studies indicate that second marriages have a higher rate of intermarriage than do first marriages. They also have a higher rate of divorce, regardless of their religious makeup. Since most second marriages do not yield children, interfaith couples often feel freer to marry—and at an earlier stage in the relationship—than do their younger counterparts. However, if you have divorced once, you see that it is possible to do so and survive. You may be less likely to stay in an untenable family situation. You will need to accept that interfaith relationships require compromise and work.

Often intermarried couples do not take advantage of learning from other couples' experience or even from their own previous experience. They may attribute their marital difficulties to the fact that their partner is not Jewish without really looking at the issues. Blaming a non-Jewish partner seems to be more socially acceptable (and certainly requires less soul-searching) than accepting responsibility for marital difficulties. It also seems easier on the couple to blame religious differences than to fault either partner for a failed marriage.

When There Are Children

Christian Children

Blending families is always a touchy process. It becomes more difficult when some children from a previous marriage are Jewish and children from your partner's previous marriage are not. While you can't make arbitrary decisions about the religious upbringing of children from a previous marriage, since another parent is usually involved, questions about holiday celebrations and continuing religious education have to be addressed early in the relationship. And you need to do so in a way that considers everyone's feelings.

One couple told me how they resolved their interfaith dilemma. Jack, a Jewish man, told Elizabeth, a nonpracticing Christian woman who considered herself Methodist and had no plans to convert, the following: he would bring up only Jewish children, his home had to be Jewish, and he could not abide having Christmas trees in the house. They both agreed that religion was an important ingredient in parenting and that families that tried to raise different children in different faiths or maintain a dual-faith household were making a mistake. While Elizabeth herself was not prepared to convert, she was willing to convert Kyla, her two-year-old daughter, born in a previous marriage. Kyla's biological father went along with the plan, and Kyla affirmed the decision her parents had made during her bat mitzvah. At twenty, Kyla continues to identify with Judaism.

Jewish Children

If you marry a non-Jew and bring your Jewish children into the family, your decision may affect their developing Jewish identity and your ability to nurture it for them. Ask yourself: Will you be able to nurture your Jewish children while simultaneously nurturing the Christian identity of your stepchildren? Similarly, can you ask your spouse to support your Jewish children while supporting the religious development of his or her own?

The more complicated the family system, the more chances there are for mishaps. Nevertheless, some families with complex configurations have found ways to make things work. Consider the merging of these two families: a practicing Lutheran man with two children and a practicing Jewish woman with two children. Before they married, they devised a prenuptial agreement stating that they would continue the religious education of the four preteen children in their own religions. Every Sunday morning, each parent set off with his or her respective children to Hebrew school or church, and they met later for lunch as a family. The entire family often attended Saturday synagogue services and extra church activities. Carefully planned holiday practices required a great deal of flexibility on the part of each family member. In the family's Passover kitchen, for example, they reserved a small, isolated area for the two Christian children to eat bread. Recently, the stepfather served as a groomsman at his stepson's Jewish wedding and led the entire assembly in the *hamotzi* blessing before the reception. In reflecting on their ability to maintain such a delicately balanced household, they both tell us that their first marriages ended in painful divorces that deeply affected their children. They were committed to making sure that their second marriages worked.

Younger Children

When younger children are part of a late-life second marriage, many parents can be involved. As you make religious decisions for these children, you will need to consider the wishes of your former partner (if they're your children) or your new partner's former partner (if they're his or her children). Family courts sometimes direct these decisions after a divorce and custody agreement. If you have no control over the arrangements, particularly when they affect your partner's children and not your own, you need to be sure you can unconditionally accept any decisions that were made. Otherwise, they will become a growing source of tension and potential conflict between you and your partner, creating an unhealthy setting for your children.

Grown Children

When parents marry a second time, children are often grown and out of the house. Decisions about children that were important to your first marriage may no longer seem relevant. Yet, adult children do voice their opinions as peers, and they expect you to heed them. Just as you may feel that your children's decisions reflect on you, they may feel that your decisions affect them. Even though children are grown, they are still part of the family that surrounds the marriage and therefore needs to be dealt with. Sam, a man who intermarried after his children were out of the house, told us quite frankly, "Were the children still in the house, I would not have done it. It was difficult enough. But I had to learn to be flexible, too. I couldn't make unreasonable demands on Jennifer's grown children and her grandchildren."

PARENTS

Although your parents now have less influence on you, your decisions will still affect your relationship with them. Independent adults you may be, but your parents will still consider themselves to be your guardians and protectors. One woman told me, "I dated John for ten years. My kids were grown and even encouraged us to marry. My parents never said anything negative about John, but I still waited until my parents died before we actually married." But another woman told me, "Although my parents died many years ago, I promised that I would honor their wish that I would not marry someone who wasn't Jewish. That is why it was so important for me that Bill converted to Judaism before we married."

Tips

1. While you may be a mature adult, the decisions you make still affect your relationships with family members, particularly your children and parents. Discuss your potential plans early in your relationship.

2. After the death of a spouse or a divorce, give yourself time to grieve and heal so that you are in a better position to clarify the issues in your interfaith relationship and make decisions about them.

3. Interfaith issues in second marriages can be more complicated than in first marriages because of the number of people involved. Be prepared to work with your partner on any issue that emerges from religious conflict before it grows too large to resolve. Consider all interfaith issues and their possible resolutions before you decide to marry.

9

SPECIAL INTERFAITH SITUATIONS

The Jewish community has become aware of the growing number of multiracial families in its midst and the need to respond to them. Similarly, the community has become more welcoming of gay and lesbian families. As the number of these families grows, so do their needs and their impact on the community. While there is still work to be done in making the Jewish community more inclusive of these groups, it is still more the case for those families that are also interfaith. Some even use the term "double jeopardy" to refer to the situation in which these special interfaith families find themselves.

By including this brief "special situations" chapter, we want to raise consciousness about the interfaith challenges facing these families and speak directly to them. We do so in part to make sure that the challenges that confront you as a member of a multiracial, gay, or lesbian family do not eclipse any attendant interfaith issues. The interfaith aspect of your relationship is another feature that may seem to set your family apart from the community. If you are a member of one of these families, your relationship to the Jewish community may be more complicated as a result.

While sociologists tend to group interfaith families together as one category, we understand that their specific constellation significantly determines the issues they face. It also determines the guidance we can offer about how to deal with challenges as they emerge. As with previous chapters, our comments are directed to the Jewish partner in the relationship but necessarily relate to other family members, as well. Some issues faced by special family groupings will reflect the social phenomenon of being multiracial or gay or lesbian, but make no mistake: they will concern interfaith matters as well.

As a partner in a multiracial or gay or lesbian marriage, you have also—intentionally or not—taken on the challenge to break down social barriers and prejudice in the community. As an interfaith couple with a Jewish identity, you are bringing this challenge to the Jewish community as well. It may be difficult for you to untangle other people's reactions to your relationship. The issues can get blurred. For example, when parents say, "She's not Jewish," the larger concern might be "She's not white." But they're reluctant to say that outright. Historically, Jews have been at the forefront of the civil rights and gay rights movements. The precedent is there. But politics change when a situation becomes personal—which creates challenges for you.

MULTIRACIAL INTERFAITH FAMILIES

While a couple that adopts a child from a different race technically forms a multiracial or interracial family, the term usually refers to couples whose partners are of different racial origins. Sometimes this includes two born Jews. After the mass immigration of Jews from Ethiopia, for example, Israel has seen a rise in the number of multiracial families. In most cases in North America, however, multiracial couples are also interfaith couples (although some partners do convert to Judaism before or upon marriage). They are less frequently formed with a Jewish partner of color who emigrated from another country.

The idea of social visibility is among the most challenging for multiracial families. The old jokes that turn on the line "Funny, you don't look Jewish" just aren't funny. This is particularly true when they take the form of exclusion. A Chinese-American woman told me that when she and her family moved into their new community, they went *shul* shopping. They were looking for a religious community that would welcome their family, and she hoped to find other families like her own. When she entered one synagogue with her husband, no one said a word to her. Although she was disappointed, she was somewhat relieved, since that meant that no one saw them as "different." However, when her husband left her momentarily, several women—who apparently had not seen her come in with her husband—approached her and asked, "May I help you?" She reflected, "They weren't here to 'welcome' me. It wouldn't have occurred to them that *I* was there for Shabbat services." She was more disappointed about being treated like a lost non-Jew than a Jew of color.

One Korean man, married to a Jewish woman, told me of his strategy in dealing with the issue of social visibility. Even though he is not Jewish, he makes sure that he wears a Jewish star or some other piece of identifying jewelry when he is in Jewish social or religious contexts, particularly with his spouse. He claims that it does not prevent all of the uninvited comments, but it does limit them. He also says that it takes some of the pressure off his wife and son. People quickly perceive him as Jewish. Thus, there seem to be fewer curious looks and fewer questions.

Some families find it helpful to seek precedents in Jewish history for their life situation. That desire no doubt motivated well-known Orthodox feminist Blu Greenberg to join with African-American Christian activist Linda Tarry to prepare a children's book, *Solomon and the Queen of Sheba,* about the biblical relationship between those two people. There are other historical precedents. For example, Moses' second wife was described as a Cushite woman, known to be black and from an African tribe. Families of color find these historical precedents affirming.

Other multiracial families find it helpful to join groups whose members are also multiracial, such as the Jewish Multiracial Network, which holds regular programs and retreats for multiracial Jewish families throughout the Boston–Washington corridor. The organization is in the process of rolling out some of its programs to a larger geographic area. Its programs encourage mentoring relationships in which experienced couples can help newly formed couples. It also presents opportunities for children to become part of a peer group of similar kids.

Families also find it helpful to share advice about how to manage their relationships with their own parents. Scott, who has done some work with the Network, speaks from his own awareness: "I have experienced first hand the social stigma of interracial dating: the nasty looks, the verbal insults. But one particularly hurtful episode came not long after my college graduation. My parents actually told me to *un*invite the African-American woman I had fallen in love with, and whom I had invited home to visit my family. They would not condone our relationship by letting her sleep under their roof. Their panic hurt their relationship with me, not mine with my girlfriend. But later, when my younger brother invited his *white* non-Jewish girlfriend home from college for a weekend, they had no problem with that!" He admits that the relationship with his parents changed that weekend. He and they are no longer as close as they once were. However, he continues to work toward repairing the rift, as he helps educate them to be more open to people of color.

Partners from different racial backgrounds have often been brought up in religions other than Christianity, such as Hinduism or Islam. While this may allow the couple to avoid the familiar "December dilemma," other religious issues emerge, particularly since their religions do not share common roots or practices.

It is also important to look at your relationship from the perspective of your partner's family. The challenge of race relations remains a struggle for both the black and the Jewish communities, in particular. As a result, your partner's family may not be as welcoming as both you and your partner hope. One black man who was married to a Jewish woman told me that his grandmother had once worked for a Jewish family who treated her poorly. As a result, she had ill feelings toward Jews in general. This negative attitude was passed down to his mother. She said to him, "How could you marry someone who treated your grandmother that way?"

GAY AND LESBIAN INTERFAITH FAMILIES

If the increase in intermarriage is partially a result of the scarcity of Jewish partners in particular populations, then it is logical for there to be a larger number of interfaith families in the gay and lesbian Jewish community than in the heterosexual Jewish community, particularly in smaller communities where there are fewer Jews. Thus, the partnering of gay and lesbian Jews with gay and lesbian non-Jews is inevitable—resulting in an even higher interfaith marriage rate in this population. One might think that the larger number of interfaith relationships in the gay community makes it easier for interfaith gay families. However, it is just as difficult for them. Perhaps that is why many gay and lesbian Jews segregate themselves from the mainstream Jewish community. Some form their own synagogues. However, not all gay synagogues are welcoming of interfaith couples. This takes many couples by surprise, as they expect an inclusive community for gays and lesbians to be inclusive for all.

It may also be disconcerting for gay couples to find among some Reform and Reconstructionist rabbis a willingness to officiate at gay and lesbian weddings—something both movements have affirmed—but outright refusal to do so for interfaith couples, gay or otherwise. These rabbis separate their perspectives on issues of social justice from those relating to Jewish continuity.

One gay practicing Jew laments that he has to go alone for services on Friday night to the local gay *shul* because his non-Jewish partner just does not feel welcome there. Before he came out of the closet, he dated a Jewish man. He had to go to the synagogue alone then, too, because they were afraid of being seen together. Now that he is openly gay, he is frustrated to find himself in a similar predicament. He says, "I don't need any more pain in my life," and he is thinking about dropping out of the synagogue entirely.

Carol, who is in a long-term lesbian relationship with Michelle, thought that converting could take the pressure off her relationship with Michelle, particularly from Michelle's family. Ultimately, however, she converted as a result of her own spiritual search. Michelle's parents had never spoken much about her lesbian partners—until Carol. Michelle's parents and many others thought Carol had converted "just for Michelle." But what really surprised Carol were the comments made by the other candidates for conversion with whom she studied. "Why bother, since you aren't going to have children?" "Do you think this will make your relationship with Michelle more permanent?" "Do you think your relationship will be seen as more 'married-like'?" And then there were comments with barely disguised aggression: *These* relationships don't usually last very long, so what's the point?" and "Michelle's Judaism isn't worth converting for." Carol was certain that people felt questioning her homosexuality was considered to be politically incorrect, so they attacked her sexual orientation through her desire to convert to Judaism.

Tips

1. Be sure you separate out the interfaith issues in your relationship from those that might be multiracial, multiethnic, or gay or lesbian.

2. Establish open lines of communication with members of your family so that you can deal with these issues one at a time.

10

The Option of Conversion

While other chapters in this volume are directed primarily to the Jewish partner in an interfaith relationship, this chapter is an introduction to conversion for non-Jewish partners who may be considering this option. Resources are included at the end of this book for those interested in exploring this issue further.

A Note About Conversion for Jewish Partners

There are many things that the Jewish partner should understand about conversion. First, it is an involved, often life-changing process. Some converts report that their Jewish partners tell them conversion is silly or not necessary, or actually attempt to dissuade them from converting. If your partner makes the decision to convert, she or he will want, and need, your support. A partner's conversion to Judaism implies an active commitment to Judaism and its practice. The only real way to share the spiritual riches of Judaism with your partner is for you to make it an important part of your own life.

HISTORICAL PERSPECTIVES ON CONVERSION

There have always been converts to Judaism, starting with the biblical Abraham and Sarah, who were themselves converts. According to a midrash, they actively sought out others to join them on their religious journey—an approach that informed much of early Jewish history. In the Bible, the term for convert is *ger* (literally, stranger). This was a broadly used term for those who were not born as Jews but who lived within the Jewish community. Conversion usually occurred as a result of marriage (which at the time had no accompanying formal ceremony or ritual). No actual process for conversion is described in the Torah. People became Jews simply by living as Jews and by casting their lot with the Jewish people. The fact is that these "strangers" were just accepted into the community. And after a generation, their origins outside the Jewish community were forgotten.

The uncomplicated nature of this "conversion process" probably explains why the Bible does not make such a big deal when its heroes marry outside their community. Later, the Rabbis felt the need to call attention to these intermarriages. Since they couldn't rewrite the stories, the Rabbis turned these "strangers" into converts *par excellence* by inserting unknown details of their lives from their rabbinic perspective. For example, Jethro, the Midian priest who was Moses' father-in-law, and Ruth became role models for converts to emulate. Ruth's poetic words to her mother-in-law, Naomi, are among the most moving lines spoken by a biblical character: "Your people shall be my people, your God, my God. Where they lodge, I shall lodge. And where they shall be buried, I too shall be buried." According to tradition, King David was descended from Ruth; since the Messiah is supposed to descend from the lineage of David, so will the Messiah. This shows how important converts are to the core of Judaism.

In time, the Jewish community slowly closed its ranks, fearful that "spies" might be among those who sought out conversion. The Jewish people learned that they had reason to be skeptical of some who sought to join them, particularly during what is called the intertestamental, or early Christian, period. People joined their community and then shared what they learned with the Roman authorities, who used the information to find the community's vulnerabilities. As a result, Rabbis were instructed to discourage people who were interested in Judaism by turning them away three times before inviting them to study for conversion. The Rabbis assumed that a sincere, serious seeker would not take no for an answer, even if given repeatedly. Yet, these same Rabbis taught that converts to Judaism were equal in all ways to born Jews (and were in some cases deemed even more "righteous"). Further, they taught that converts were never to be reminded of their former status as non-Jews. It is this mixed message that some rabbis have continued to give.

Personally, I have learned more "Torah" from converts to Judaism than I have from born Jews. I am often struck by the depth of their faith and commitment to Judaism—and their ability to be open to such transformation in their lives. I am impressed by their courage to make such drastic personal changes and their enthusiasm about Judaism. Each time I hold the Torah in my hands, I feel that I am personally at Sinai. And when I give the Torah to a convert and ask him or her to become at one with it, I too am transformed. When I travel to Israel, I like to travel with those new to the land so that I can experience it fresh each time. Similarly, as wonderful as it is to celebrate Judaism with those who are familiar with its practices, it is awe-inspiring for me to celebrate its many rites and rituals with those who do not have a storehouse of Jewish memories. To see the glow of the Sabbath candles reflected in the eyes of converts to Judaism for the first time in their lives is to directly experience the light of the Divine.

It is rather common to hear Jewish leaders say that all Jews today are "Jews-by-choice" (a term commonly used today instead of "convert" or the more prosaic term of "proselyte"). This means we are each forced to make Jewish choices daily, regardless of whether we were born as Jews, chose Judaism on our own, or were first exposed to it because we fell in love with someone who was Jewish.

WHAT IS CONVERSION?

A conversion is a religious act. The conversion itself is a ceremony in which a person publicly and ritually declares allegiance to a new faith and, in the process, makes a clear separation from a former faith. I believe that there are really two levels to conversion. The first is fixed in time and determined by ritual. This level can be easily controlled and put on a calendar. The second, which is far more important, is a conversion of the heart. It is internal, and it is not marked by time or place or ritual. It is not unusual for it to take place years before you are ready for the formal ritual.

While there may be some slight variations as to what is specifically required, the formal Jewish conversion ritual includes: study, *milah* (ritual circumcision for males), *mikvah* (immersion in a ritual bath), and certification by a *bet din* (rabbinical court). For males who have been surgically circumcised previously, the remaining foreskin is simply pricked in order to produce a droplet of blood (the *tipat dam*).

The inner conversion of the heart is harder to describe or provide guidance for. One convert told me that her real conversion took place in her mother-in-law's kitchen: "That's where I really became a Jew," she says. There her mother-in-law shared family lore as well as holiday recipes that were family favorites. Sometimes, the inner conversion can be identified only in retrospect, when a particular event makes you suddenly realize that you are Jewish. It often occurs when something happens in Israel and you understand that you have become part of the Jewish people. Sometimes this happens before the formal ceremony of conversion. Sometimes it happens after the interview with the *bet din* (rabbinic court). And sometimes it doesn't happen at all.

Unfortunately, not all conversions are regarded equal. While the Reform movement generally accepts the conversions of the other movements, the other movements generally do not reciprocate. Each movement sets its own standards for conversions. Orthodox rabbis tend not to accept conversions by Reform, Reconstructionist, and

Conservative rabbis because of the positions that they hold on other issues.

WILL I LOSE HIM OR HER IF I DON'T CONVERT?

As a non-Jew who is in love with someone who is Jewish, you may fear losing your partner if you do not convert. This may happen if your partner feels strongly about it and would not consider marriage under any other circumstances. This attitude often prolongs the engagement period (which is already longer among interfaith couples than for couples who share the same religion). Sometimes the position taken by the Jewish partner leads to the dissolution of a relationship (or a decision not to marry) when the non-Jewish partner chooses not to convert. But make sure that "religion," and not other unaddressed problems, is really what is preventing the relationship from going forward.

It takes a great deal of inner strength to convert to another faith, particularly when that faith may not be celebrated with the same intensity in the family into which you are marrying as was the religion of your own parents. It takes courage to educate children in a new religion if that is your responsibility. But this challenge often leads to greater commitment.

Those who marry but don't convert may experience more difficulty in finding their place within families and the organized Jewish community, particularly if they enter a not-very-welcoming family or a not-so-inclusive Jewish community. While conversion will not solve all problems, it can give a couple more common ground. Sometimes it causes other problems, too, as when it assumes a wholesale renunciation of interests and desires. One of Joan's friends told her that when he was introduced to his future mother-in-law, she looked at her daughter and said, "He is going to be a good boy and do what we talked about. Isn't he?" He doesn't regret his conversion, but he is tired of the family assuming that he did it to satisfy their wishes and not his own desires.

Conversion, for many, is an important step in a spiritual journey.

We also think that conversion is good for the Jewish people. But we don't believe it is the only route for people. So don't be surprised if a rabbi does not encourage you to convert. It may be a holdover from the tradition requiring the rabbi to say "no" three times before welcoming a potential convert. Or it may be that he or she wants you to make a decision that is best for you—and for your partner. The decision to convert should be weighed carefully. If your partner persuades you to convert, he or she may worry during the entire course of your relationship whether that was right, or fair, to do. Nevertheless, couples have to be made aware that traditional Jewish law will not accept as valid a nonconversionary marriage between a Jew and a non-Jew. As a result, these traditional Jewish laws do not recognize the children of such a union as legitimate. Therefore, a nonconversionary marriage will be met with disdain by the traditional segments of the Jewish community, though by no means all of the Jewish community.

What Difference Will It Make?

When you speak to a rabbi about the possibility of conversion, you will have an opportunity to raise any religious questions you may have. However, there are some practical implications you may also want to think about. If you convert to Judaism, you may avoid many of the basic challenges faced by interfaith couples as they plot a course through the myriad of synagogue rites and rituals, particularly regarding life-cycle events (see chapter 6). If you convert before having children, there will be fewer questions about the status of your children in the community. You will be able to hand the Torah to your future children during the bar or bat mitzvah ceremony—a common custom in many liberal synagogues today. And you will be able to stand with them under their wedding canopy one day—something that many rabbis will not permit if you don't convert. And although no one wants to speak of death, if you convert there will be no question about being buried in a Jewish cemetery.

THE PROCESS OF CONVERSION

Conversion is long and demanding. The lengthy process usually unfolds in this manner:

- Upon recognizing the desire to formalize a conversion, an individual may contact a rabbi. In Judaism, a rabbi is not an intermediary between God and humankind. Rather, the rabbi is a teacher who transmits Jewish tradition and values, and who sets the standards which must be embraced by those seeking to convert. The rabbi may, as in times past, dissuade the candidate to test his or her commitment. (The tradition, according to the great twelfth-century sage Maimonides, is to "draw close with the right hand and discourage with the left.")

- If the person is still interested in pursuing this path, the rabbi may recommend weekly classes, either in a group or on an individual basis. These may last several months or longer.

  These classes consist of intensive discussion, probing, reading. Sometimes, students may read as many as fifty books or more. In conjunction with learning about Jewish history, customs, traditions and ceremonies and reading about the *mitzvot* (613 commandments in the Torah), some time is ordinarily devoted to studying the Hebrew language.

- Students attend worship services and congregational programs and gradually incorporate Judaism into their daily lives. Concurrent with all this, candidates meet regularly with their host rabbi, who monitors and encourages their spiritual development.

- At the conclusion of this process, the candidate for conversion may write a spiritual autobiography and even take a written test.

In the Orthodox and Conservative movements, the candidate meets with a *bet din,* a "court" of three rabbis. The *bet din* affirms the candidate's readiness and "authorizes" the actual conversion. Following this, the candidate is immersed in the *mikvah,* a ritual pool of water. By completely submersing oneself in the water and then reciting the appropriate liturgy, the *mikvah* immersion symbolizes the spiritual transformation of the soul. For male candidates, entrance into the covenant of Abraham includes circumcision. For those already circumcised, the ritual of *hatafat dam brit,* the taking of a tiny drop of blood from the penis, is performed as a symbolic circumcision.

Standards within the Reform and Reconstructionist movements vary from one congregation to the next. The Reform and Reconstructionist movements require that candidates for conversion declare acceptance of the Jewish faith and people before three adult witnesses, at least one of whom must be a rabbi. Although these movements have not, in the past, required that candidates for conversion undergo *hatafat dam brit,* this ritual may be required by individual Reform and Reconstructionist rabbis, and increasingly more rabbis are doing so. The Reconstructionist movement requires that the candidate for conversion be immersed in a *mikvah,* while the Reform movement does not set this as a requirement. Immersion in *mikvah* and *hatafat dam brit,* when not required by the sponsoring rabbi, may be chosen by the convert to further ritualize his/her conversion experience.

At conversion, a Hebrew name is bestowed upon the candidate to symbolize one's new identity. There is often a ceremony of welcome in the sanctuary before the open Ark. The newly converted Jew is handed the Torah and then recites a pledge of loyalty to Judaism. This includes the *Sh'ma Yisrael,* the statement of God's unity. The rabbi may also recite the three-fold priestly benediction—a traditional blessing for the well-being of the Jewish people.

The pledge of loyalty recited by the candidate usually reads as follows:

Of my own free will, I choose to enter the eternal Covenant between God and the people of Israel and to become a Jew. I accept Judaism to the exclusion of all other religious faiths and practices. Under all circumstances, I will be loyal to the Jewish people and to Judaism. I promise to establish a Jewish home and to participate actively in the life of the synagogue and of the Jewish community. I commit myself to the pursuit of Torah and Jewish knowledge. If I should be blessed with children, I promise to raise them as Jews.

THE STATUS OF CHILDREN

Jewish law is often complicated, and it is best to review its details with your sponsoring rabbi. Generally, if your partner is a Jewish woman, then traditional Judaism will not require you to convert your children, regardless of your status. This is called matrilineal descent. Reform and Reconstructionist Judaism affirm patrilineal descent, as well. This means that the child of a Jewish father (regardless of the religious status of the mother) is presumed to be Jewish. However, this presumption must be affirmed through naming, *brit milah,* and Jewish education, and the child cannot be entered into or schooled in another religion. Sometimes liberal Jews take their cues from Orthodox Judaism when making decisions and convert their children even when they may be considered Jewish under the prin ciple of patrilineal descent. While some may feel that this is inconsistent with the way they live their lives, this is really more of a halakhic challenge of sorts, rather than an ideological one. (*Halakha* is the term for Jewish law.) Some liberal Jews think that if they follow the legal principles of Orthodoxy, they will encounter fewer problems in the future. For some, it is helpful to look at these legal requirements as a means of affirmation, rather than part of the process of conversion.

Bearing this is mind, if you are a woman and you convert before the birth of your children, your children need not convert in order to be Jewish. If you convert after the birth of your children, then they must undergo conversion, too. The requirements for such conversion are tailored to the age of the child. Often their education is handled through enrollment in the synagogue's religious school. If they are under the age for bar or bat mitzvah, they must affirm their religious status through this ceremonial rite of passage when they become of Jewish legal age. The same holds true for children who are adopted or come into the family via a second marriage and were not born to Jewish parents. Anne Littman, Joan's younger daughter, reflects on her conversion with *mikvah* at age seven, seeing it as a special way she connects to Judaism as a Jewish woman. "I knew I was Jewish, but maybe now I am a little bit more Jewish, and I have had an experience many Jewish women have only read about."

MAKING THE PERSONAL DECISION

Conversion to Judaism is your decision, and it is an opportunity open to you at any time during your life. Some people find that while they may not have been exposed to Judaism before their relationship with someone who is Jewish, the religion fulfills a spiritual longing that they had felt for many years and didn't know how to satisfy. Others who are open to the Jewish mystical tradition believe that they were Jewish in a previous life and are now returning to their religious roots. Joan recently met a woman interested in conversion. After exploring her family tree with her, it turned out that her maternal grandmother had been Jewish.

As you make your decision, and as you consider your own needs and those of your partner and future children, take into consideration the feelings of your own parents. They may not understand your decision or may feel that you have abandoned them and the way they brought you up. These are normal feelings. Some people feel unable to convert to Judaism while their own parents are still alive, fearful of hurting them or afraid that their conversion will be perceived as rejection or betrayal.

Converts have explained to me that various events in their lives motivated them to make the decision to convert. One woman even told me that her decision was confirmed when she was watching a commercial film with a Jewish theme. In the midst of a synagogue post-conversion study group, one man said that his conversion was prompted by the death of his wife's uncle. While sharing with his wife and her family in mourning this beloved uncle, he decided that he wanted to make sure that he would be buried with his wife and her family. His wife was puzzled, and she told her story: "I will never understand how a funeral could motivate him to convert when our wedding and the birth of our three children was not motivation enough." And yet, this particular event sparked an awareness of his needs.

ASKING YOUR PARTNER TO CONVERT

Jewish partners often want to ask their non-Jewish partners to convert but are unsure how to do so. Perhaps it is their own ambivalence. Perhaps it is their own feelings of inadequacy about Judaism and Jewish knowledge. It might be plain lack of interest. Ironically, it is not uncommon for Jewish partners to be the greatest obstacles to conversion. It may seem odd, but you may have to help your Jewish partner encourage you to convert! Use your conversion as an opportunity to learn together, to become more intimate with one another by exploring things in life that really matter. Together you can find your place in Jewish history, and in the greater Jewish family and community. We welcome you.

Tips

1. Develop a relationship with a rabbi whom you trust, someone with whom you can discuss your concerns regarding conversion, and who can guide you through the conversion process—and afterwards.

2. Ask your Jewish partner to take the journey with you. It will be indispensable to your evolving relationship, your ability to establish a Jewish home, and the opportunities to establish Jewish memories for your children.

3. Make the most of the conversion experience. Celebrate it fully with your friends and family. Be proud of your decision to join the Jewish people, making its destiny your own.

EPILOGUE:
INTERFAITH
MARRIAGE AS A
JOURNEY

When I counsel an interfaith couple contemplating marriage, I always ask them to imagine what their life together will look like in five, ten, and twenty years. These pictures vary greatly. While no one can predict the future, and many things—positive and negative—give direction to our personal journeys, it is important for partners to hear each other's dreams. This is particularly important because the future that couples imagine as adults is often different from what they pictured as their adult lives when they were children, or even a few years earlier. It is also helpful for me to hear what each partner has to say aloud, so that I can identify for them what issues are yet to be resolved before they make a long-term commitment to each other.

In my conversations, I have found that some families resent being called an interfaith couple or an interfaith family. Couples figure that if they have made Jewish choices in their lives, if the religion of the household is Jewish, then they are not "interfaith." This is particularly true for those who have lived in the Jewish community as a Jewish family for many years. For some, including many in the Jewish community, an interfaith relationship will always be classified as an interfaith relationship—even after they have worked out its various challenges, even after the kids are grown and settled on their own, even after they have gotten into a familiar and comfortable routine as a Jewish family. During a recent conversation I had with an interfaith couple who had been married twenty years, Jack's comments about religious identity surprised his wife. Although they had brought up two Jewish boys, and Jack had left the practice of Catholicism at the same time he left his parents' home to go to college, he still considered *himself* a Roman Catholic. However, he had never thought of their family as interfaith. But when I later spoke to their congregational rabbi, he certainly considered them to be an interfaith family.

Even if your partner converts, whether early in your relationship or later on, issues needing to be addressed can still come up after many years of marriage. This may sound harsh or even contradictory, since Jewish law recognizes a Jew-by-choice as equal to one who was born into Judaism. And the Reform and Reconstructionist Jewish movements are explicit about their desire to welcome interfaith families. However, these residual concerns may have more to do with your relationship to family members than with the Jewish community. Such issues don't go away on their own, and time may not diminish them. They may surface when you discover, just as we all do, gaps in your Jewish background and the knowledge needed to help your children develop their Jewish identity. They may come up unexpectedly in the midst of a relative's celebration. And it may be that your partner will never know enough to satisfy some members of your family. Similarly, *you* may never be "Jewish enough" for them from this point forward; after all, "You made the decision to marry a non-Jew!" Be forewarned: only in unusual circumstances do they know as much as you think they know, or as much as they profess to know. Just study now with your partner, and continue to do so. That's what really matters.

Sam, a non-Jewish partner, framed it this way. In reflecting on his relationship with Susan's parents, he told us: "After so many years, they have at this point accepted me as a good person and a loving husband and father, so I can relax. I don't feel I have to defend myself any longer. I don't feel I have to be on guard. In turn, I have come to see them as such decent good people—something that I could never see before. I can now say to myself 'You know, I wouldn't mind if my daughter grew up to be like these people.'"

As you move forward you will encounter others who have gone the same way before you, who can be of help. In the Jewish community, there are advocates of the intermarried who can provide you with support. As you get to know your local community, consider who besides your partner—perhaps especially besides your partner—can be of help to you.

Some synagogues sponsor groups that encourage contact with "younger" couples (those just starting out on their journey) and "older" couples (those who have been in an intermarried relationship for five years or more). But this distinction has nothing to do with age. It is about the accumulated interfaith experiences of a couple. Some experiences may come from interaction with the community through your non-Jewish partner. Look for these groups in your local community, and join them. Joan continues to be active in her synagogue's interfaith couples group after many years of participation. After hearing that a synagogue-sponsored meeting for interfaith couples was going to be held at the Littman home, a relative newcomer to the group innocently remarked, "I didn't know that Larry Littman wasn't Jewish." (Of course, it was Joan who was not born Jewish!)

The more we learn, the more we discover how much we don't know—even after living a Jewish family life (convert to Judaism or not) for many years. But the feelings of "otherness" don't always go away. Joan reminds us, "I still get scared, after living a Jewish life all of these years. I recently walked into a Jewish day school in the community in a swarm of teenage boys wearing *yarmulkes*. They all gave me *the look,* which I interpreted as 'What is *she* doing here?'— what I have come to call my '*goyim* alert.' Later I came to understand that they were simply curious, wondering what I, an unfamiliar face, was doing at their school." It's easy to be defeated and feel afraid, to feel that you may never "get it," and disengage as a result. But it is far better to be motivated now and prepare for the life ahead of you. Rather than seeing the "long road" as a "long haul," join us as we see it, as a road filled with opportunity and joy.

Here, classical Judaism has something important to teach us. The Passover experience, which really shaped the mindset of the Jewish people, including the expansive notion of welcoming the stranger in our midst, emphasizes one idea: optimism. In the midst of the experience of going back into Egypt, into the "narrow places" (the literal definition of *Mitzrayim* or Egypt) of our lives, we are reminded that the possibility of freedom and renewal is always present. As the Rabbis liked to say, we could not have experienced the liberation of the Exodus had we not gone down into Egypt. The road ahead for you as an interfaith couple is a continuation of the journey our people took through the desert. It will have its "bitter waters." But know, just as our ancient ancestors realized, you *can* reach the Promised Land. What it will take to get there is up to you and your partner. May God bless you along the way.

RESOURCES

CONVERSION

CCAR Committee on *Gerut* (Conversion)
Central Conference of American Rabbis (Reform Judaism)
192 Lexington Avenue
New York, NY 10016
(212) 684-4990

RRA Commission on *Gerut* (Conversion)
Reconstructionist Rabbinical Association
Church Road and Greenwood Avenue
Wyncote, PA 19095
(215) 576-5210

RA Committee on *Keruv* (Outreach)
Rabbinical Assembly (Conservative Judaism)
3080 Broadway
New York, NY 10027
(212) 678-8060

RCA Commission on *Gerut* (Conversion)
Rabbinical Council of America (Orthodox Judaism)
305 Seventh Avenue
New York, NY 10001
(212) 807-9042

INTERFAITH COUPLES AND FAMILIES

Jewish Outreach Institute
1270 Broadway, Suite 609
New York, NY 10001
(212) 760-1440
www.joi.org

InterfaithFamily.com, Inc.
P.O. Box 9129
90 Oak St.
Newton Upper Falls, MA 02464
(617) 965-7700
www.interfaithfamily.com

MOHALIM (RITUAL CIRCUMCISERS)

Berit Milah Board of Reform Judaism/National Organization of
  American Mohalim
Hebrew Union College-Jewish Institute of Religion
3077 University Avenue
Los Angeles, CA 90007
(800) 899-0925

NOTES

CHAPTER 1

1. Susan Weidman Schneider, *Intermarriage: The Challenge of Living with Differences Between Christians and Jews.* New York: The Free Press, 1989, p. 3.

2. Rachel Cowan, *Moment,* Vol. 15, No. 2 (April 1990), p. 14.

CHAPTER 2

1. Samuel Sandmel, *When a Jew and Christian Marry.* Philadelphia: Fortress Press, 1977, p. 25.

2. Esther Perel, "Communication In and About Intermarriage" in *The Imperatives of Jewish Outreach,* Egon Mayer, ed. New York: Jewish Outreach Institute, 1991, p. 144.

CHAPTER 10

1. Allan L. Berkowitz and Patti Moskovitz, *Embracing the Covenant: Converts to Judaism Talk About Why and How.* Woodstock, Vt.: Jewish Lights Publishing, 1996, pp. 115–117.

GLOSSARY

Ahashuerus: Non-Jewish king of ancient Persia, who figures prominently in the Purim story as the husband of Queen Esther.

Aramaic: Semitic language that flourished from the seventh through the fourth centuries B.C.E. and is closely related to Hebrew. It was once the *lingua franca* for Jews. Key sacred texts and prayers were written in Aramaic, and we still say them in Aramaic today.

bar/bat mitzvah: The ceremony which marks the religious coming of age for boys (bar mitzvah) at thirteen and for girls (bat mitzvah, sometimes written as bas mitzvah) at twelve, following which they become responsible for their actions and religious obligations.

bet din: Rabbinical court, made up of three rabbis.

bimah: Raised platform in the front of a synagogue sanctuary.

brit milah (sometimes referred to as *bris*): Literally, "the covenant of ritual circumcision," for a boy, on the eighth day of life. This ritual is performed by one who is trained and certified (called a *mohel*) or a physician trained by the Jewish community to combine the ritual elements and medical practice, often assisted by a local rabbi. Also called *milah* (circumcision).

chuppah: Wedding canopy.

Elul: Month on the Hebrew calendar that occurs in late summer, or early fall, just before the High Holy Days. It is a month of introspection and self-reflection, marked by the daily recitation of Psalm 27, and culminates in the reading of *selichot,* prayers of supplication.

ger: Literally, "stranger," Hebrew term for male convert.

giyyuret: Female convert.

goyim (plural; *goy,* singular): A term that literally means "nations" but has come to refer to all non-Jews, often used in a derogatory fashion.

Haggadah: Prayer book guide for the Passover *seder* that provides the narrative story of the Israelites' experience of slavery in Egypt, their Exodus, and their journey in the desert.

Halakha: Literally, "the way," term used to refer to the body of Jewish law.

hamantaschen: Cookie-like triangular pastry served at Purim. It is a pun on the Yiddish word *mahn* (poppy) and *taschen* (pastry pockets) and the name of the central villain in the Purim story: Haman. Called *oznei-Haman* (literally, Haman's ears) in Hebrew.

hamotzi: Literally, "the One who brings forth," namely, God; this is the blessing said before meals when bread is eaten.

Hanukkah: From the Hebrew word "rededication," the winter festival that occurs in late November or December and celebrates the rededication of the ancient Temple in Jerusalem after the defeat of the Assyrian-Greeks by a small band of Jews called the Maccabees, led by Judah.

Hillel: Influential rabbi who lived in the first century B.C.E.

ketubah: Traditional marriage agreement certificate.

matzah: Flat unleavened bread, the central symbol during the holiday of Passover (*Pesach* in Hebrew). Made without leavening because it was hastily prepared and carried when the Israelites left Egypt after their deliverance from slavery in the ancient world (about 1250 B.C.E.).

menorah (also called *hanukkiah*): Specially designed candelabrum for ritual use during Hanukkah. Adapted from the *menorah* in the ancient Temple of Jerusalem, which had seven candles, one for each day of creation, Hanukkah *menorot* (plural of *menorah*) have eight branches, symbolizing the eight days of the holiday of rededication. A ninth candle, termed a server candle, or *shamash*, is used to light the other eight.

mezuzah: Literally, "doorpost," now referring to the scroll and its case that is affixed to the doorpost. This includes specific texts from the Torah (including the *shema* blessing and surrounding blessings that instruct us to, in fact, affix the *mezuzah*). The *mezuzah* helps to identify a Jewish house as one where God's presence is acknowledged.

midrash: A parable by the Rabbis that is generally designed to explicate the biblical text. It may simply be a story, or it may used to offer legal guidance as well.

mikvah: Ritual bath, used for ritual cleansing and conversion.

mitzvah (*mitzvot*, plural): "Commandments," referring to 613 sacred obligations incumbent on Jews, as directed by God. The term is often used to refer to good works or good deeds.

mohel: Person trained to do a ritual circumcision (plural, *mohalim*).

Passover (*Pesach* in Hebrew): Springtime festival that celebrates the deliverance of the ancient Israelites from Egyptian slavery.

Purim: Later winter holiday that celebrates the foiling of a plot to kill the Jews of ancient Persia.

Rosh Hashanah: Jewish New Year; occurs in the fall.

siddur: Prayer book (plural, *siddurim*).

Shabbat: The Sabbath.

Shavuot: Late spring or early summer harvest festival that celebrates the giving of the Torah on Mount Sinai.

Simchat Torah: Fall holiday, immediately following Sukkot, that is a celebration of Torah and marks the time when the weekly Torah reading is concluded for the year and begun once again.

Sukkot: Fall harvest festival marked by the construction of temporary dwellings, reminiscent of the booths used by the ancient Israelites as they wandered in the desert.

tipat dam: A symbolic drop of blood that is ritually let from the remaining foreskin for the conversion of a male who has already been surgically circumcised.

Torah: The parchment scroll on which is written the five books of Moses, the first five books of the Hebrew Scriptures.

yarmulke: Yiddish for "skullcap" (*kepah* in Hebrew), worn by Jewish men during prayer. Some cover their head for study and eating as well, and some keep their heads covered all the time. It has become increasingly popular for women to also wear *yarmulkes* or a similar head covering.

Yom Kippur: Day of Atonement, one of two so-called High Holy Days that take place in the early fall, ten days after Rosh Hashanah. It is observed by fasting and prayer.

Zohar: A mystical commentary on the Torah that is the primary source for Jewish mysticism.

BOOKS FOR FURTHER READING

EXPLAINING JEWISH TRADITION TO OUR NON-JEWISH RELATIVES

Lawrence Kushner, *Jewish Spirituality: A Brief Introduction for Christians.* Woodstock, Vt.: Jewish Lights Publishing, 2002.

Rabbi Kushner describes Judaism in such a way that people whose own tradition traces its roots to Judaism can understand and relate to it. This engaging introduction helps readers make the connection between religion, spirituality, and the everyday.

Stuart Matlins and Arthur Magida, *How to Be a Perfect Stranger, 3rd Ed.: The Essential Religious Etiquette Handbook.* Woodstock, Vt.: SkyLight Paths Publishing, 2003.

This book offers do's and don'ts, whys and wherefores for attending life-cycle and holiday events among various religious communities. It is particularly helpful for families whose members participate in a variety of religious traditions.

GENERAL INTRODUCTION TO JUDAISM

Daniel Judson and Kerry M. Olitzky, *The Rituals and Practices of a Jewish Life: A Handbook for Personal Spiritual Renewal.* Woodstock, Vt.: Jewish Lights Publishing, 2002.

This is an introductory volume for individuals who want to introduce Jewish ritual into their lives. The authors avoid any rigid

approaches to rituals and instead provide for a continuum of practices from the traditional to the more innovative. Readers will relate
to the many personal experiences that are shared by the authors and
others.

Stuart M. Matlins, ed., *The Jewish Lights Spirituality Handbook: A
Guide to Understanding, Exploring & Living a Spiritual Life.* Woodstock, Vt.: Jewish Lights Publishing, 2001.

This book offers the best spiritual teaching from among fifty of
the Jewish community's most spiritual teachers. It begins with a
simple introduction to spirituality and moves on to the more complicated nuances of spiritual understanding.

ABOUT INTERFAITH MARRIAGES

Paul and Rachel Cowan, *Mixed Blessings: Overcoming the Stumbling
Blocks in an Interfaith Marriage.* New York: Penguin, 1989.

Emerging from their own experience, Rabbi Rachel Cowan (a
Jew-by-choice) and her late husband, a former writer for the *Village
Voice,* take readers through the challenges and misgivings they con-
fronted as an intermarried couple. They provide readers with straightforward guidance and insight, noting strategies that worked for them.

Joel Crohn, *Mixed Matches: How to Create Successful Interracial,
Interethnic and Interfaith Relationships.* New York: Fawcett Books,
1995.

A primer for people involved in all kinds of relationships that
span divergent cultures, written by a psychotherapist with extensive
experience in cross-cultural counseling.

Joel Crohn, Howard J. Markman, Susan Blumberg, and Janice
R. Levine, *Beyond the Chuppah: A Jewish Guide to Happy Marriages.*
New York: John Wiley and Sons, 2001.

The authors combine the results of scientific research with the
best of Jewish tradition to promote healthy and long-lasting Jewish
and interfaith marriages. It is heavily influenced by the Prevention
and Relationship Enhancement Program (PREP), a premarital
counseling tool used by family therapists and marriage counselors.

Ronnie Friedland and Edmund Case, *The Guide to Jewish Interfaith Family Life: An InterfaithFamily.com Handbook.* Woodstock, Vt.: Jewish Lights Publishing, 2001.

This practical, inspiring book is a compilation of some of the most informative, instructional, and provocative essays that have appeared in the biweekly webzine *InterfaithFamily.com.* Edited by the editor and publisher of the webzine, it includes a preface by Rabbi Kerry M. Olitzky that puts the essays into perspective for the reader. Particularly helpful are the first-person experiences of interfaith family members' quests to create meaningful Jewish holiday experiences.

Gabrielle Glaser, *Strangers to the Tribe: Portraits of Interfaith Marriage.* Boston: Houghton Mifflin, 1997.

A compassionate and thoughtful account of eleven families who juggle issues of ethnicity, class, and religion.

Egon Mayer, *Love and Tradition: Marriage between Jews and Christians.* New York: Plenum Press, 1985.

A sociological overview of interfaith marriage based on a nationwide survey of more than four hundred couples.

Ellen J. McClain, *Embracing the Stranger: Intermarriage and the Future of the American Jewish Community.* New York: Basic Books, 1995.

The author thoughtfully argues for the inclusion of intermarried families in the Jewish community while also pointing out the flaws in the 1990 National Jewish Population Study, which prompted alarm over the rate of interfaith marriage. She suggests reasons for the tendency of interfaith couples to reject Judaism and what can be done to make the Jewish community more welcoming.

Samuel Sandmel, *When a Jew and Christian Marry.* Philadelphia: Fortress Press, 1977.

While this book is a little dated and may rely on assumptions that are no longer valid, it is an excellent resource for both members of an interfaith couple. Of particular note is its overview of Christianity for the Jewish partner and of Judaism for the Christian partner.

Susan Weidman Schneider, *Intermarriage: The Challenge of Living with Differences Between Christians and Jews.* New York: The Free Press, 1989.

While the studies cited in this book are somewhat dated, the challenges presented by the author—and through the words of couples she writes about—remain the same today as when the book was written. It is a fine blend of scholarship and popular writing.

Sanford Seltzer, *Jews and Non-Jews: Getting Married.* New York: UAHC Press, 1984.

This is an updated version of *Jews and Non-Jews: Falling in Love,* which was one of the earliest books on interfaith marriage. This brief volume addresses many issues that interfaith couples will have to face if they anticipate marriage. It assumes the perspective of the Reform movement and is primarily synagogue-focused.

Alan Silverstein, *Preserving Jewishness in Your Family: After Intermarriage Has Occurred.* Northvale, N.J.: Jason Aronson, 1995.

Written by a Conservative rabbi, who attempts to help families nurture the Jewish identity of their family members. He presents the thesis that without positive action, an intermarriage threatens to undermine the Jewish identity of all family members.

WEDDINGS

Anita Diamant, *The New Jewish Wedding,* revised edition. New York: Fireside, 2001.

This is an updated version of a classic book on Jewish wedding ritual. It speaks to all Jewish denominations and includes a chapter on interfaith weddings.

Stuart M. Matlins, *The Perfect Stranger's Guide to Wedding Ceremonies: A Guide to Etiquette in Other People's Religious Ceremonies.* Woodstock, Vt.: SkyLight Paths Publishing, 2000.

This comprehensive guide covers all the major (and many minor) denominations and religions found in North America.

ABOUT CONVERSION

David Belin, *Choosing Judaism: An Opportunity for Everyone,* revised edition. New York: Jewish Outreach Institute, 2000.

Available free of charge from the Jewish Outreach Institute, this is a brief but informative discussion about the openness of Judaism. It can also be downloaded from the Web (www.joi.org).

Allan L. Berkowitz and Patti Moskovitz, *Embracing the Covenant: Converts to Judaism Talk About Why and How.* Woodstock, Vt.: Jewish Lights Publishing, 1996.

This is a collection of personal accounts by more than twenty converts to Judaism. Many of the stories are inspiring, and they provide readers with opportunities for personal reflection on their own spiritual journeys. Appendixes provide detailed information on the process of conversion, as well as resources to help people at any stage of the process.

Anita Diamant, *Choosing a Jewish Life: A Handbook for People Converting to Judaism and for Their Family and Friends.* New York: Schocken Books, 1997.

This is a sensitive book that examines the often complex issues that emerge during the process of conversion. It combines ritual guidance with insight and practical advice.

Lawrence J. Epstein, *Conversion to Judaism: A Guidebook.* Northvale, N.J.: Jason Aronson, 1997.

For those who want an intellectual discussion of the subject of conversion, the author presents an academic approach for finding one's way to Judaism.

————, *Questions and Answers on Conversion to Judaism.* Northvale, N.J.: Jason Aronson, 1998.

A practical guide to the process of conversion and the larger issues that a person must deal with when considering becoming a Jew.

Walter Homolka, Walter Jacob, and Esther Seidel, eds., *Not by Birth Alone: Conversion to Judaism.* London: Continuum, 1997.

An overview of the spiritual, ethnic, and historical conceptions of Jewish identity, this book examines and compares theological notions of "Who is a Jew?" without any direction, instruction, or how-to.

Maurice Lamm, *Becoming a Jew.* Middle Village, N.Y.: Jonathan David Publishers, 1991.

A sensitive introduction to the Orthodox approach to conversion.

ABOUT WELCOMING CHILDREN

Anita Diamant, *The New Jewish Baby Book: Names, Ceremonies and Customs—A Guide for Today's Families,* revised edition. Woodstock, Vt.: Jewish Lights Publishing, 1994.

Like the same author's book about weddings, this book offers guidance for naming ceremonies and birthing rituals, both traditional and innovative, including specific information on how to involve non-Jewish family members and friends.

————, *Bible Baby Names: Spiritual Choices from Judeo-Christian Tradition.* Woodstock, Vt.: Jewish Lights Publishing, 1996.

An overview of 630 biblical names, with an emphasis on names that are relatively common in contemporary American society.

Debra Nussbaum Cohen, *Celebrating Your New Jewish Daughter: Creating Jewish Ways to Welcome Baby Girls into the Covenant—New and Traditional Ceremonies.* Woodstock, Vt.: Jewish Lights Publishing, 2001.

This is a comprehensive and creative volume that offers numerous options for naming and birth ceremonies for baby girls, including information specifically for interfaith families.

FOR BAR AND BAT MITZVAH

Jeffrey Salkin, *Putting God on the Guest List: How to Reclaim the Spiritual Meaning of Your Child's Bar or Bat Mitzvah* and *For Kids— Putting God on Your Guest List: How to Claim the Spiritual Meaning of Your Bar or Bat Mitzvah.* Woodstock, Vt.: Jewish Lights Publishing, 1996 and 1998.

These books give readers background on the bar and bat mitzvah ceremonies. They also suggest ways to deepen their meaning and contains specific ideas for including non-Jewish family members in the ceremony.

JEWISH PARENTING

Yosef I. Abramowitz and Susan Silverman, *Jewish Family and Life: Traditions, Holidays and Values for Today's Parents and Children.* New York: Golden Books, 1997.

An accessible and practical guide for parents that provides them with background and suggestions for celebrating Judaism with children, particularly for holidays and rituals. It also offers insights about the underlying values of Jewish celebrations and ceremonies.

Anita Diamant, *Living a Jewish Life: Jewish Traditions, Customs, and Values for Today's Families.* New York: HarperCollins, 1996.

A practical guide to incorporating Judaism into daily life.

Hayim Halevy Donin, *To Raise a Jewish Child: A Guide for Parents.* New York: Basic Books, 1991.

Written from an Orthodox point of view, this book provides extensive information on bringing up Jewish children. It will be helpful whether you are familiar with Jewish religion or a newcomer to the community.

Andrea King, *If I'm Jewish and You're Christian, What Are the Kids? A Parenting Guide for Interfaith Families.* New York: UAHC Press, 1993.

A guide that offers practical advice and suggestions for all aspects of bringing up children in a Jewish-Christian marriage.

Kerry M. Olitzky, Steven M. Rosman, and David P. Kasakove, *When Your Jewish Child Asks Why: Answers for Tough Questions.* Hoboken, N.J.: KTAV Publishing, 1993.

After collecting important questions that Jewish youngsters really wanted answered, the authors collected responses from numerous Jewish educators representing a variety of perspectives.

These responses provide parents with important guidance for answering their own children's questions.

Steven Carr Reuben, *But How Will You Raise the Children?: A Guide to Interfaith Marriage.* New York: Pocket Books, 1987.

Straight advice from a congregational rabbi who asks the hard questions and answers them in a very supportive way.

HOLIDAY BOOKS

Danielle Dardashti and Roni Sarig, *The Jewish Family Fun Book: Holiday Projects, Everyday Activities, and Travel Ideas with Jewish Themes.* Woodstock, Vt.: Jewish Lights Publishing, 2002.

With over eighty-five easy-to-do activities to reinvigorate age-old Jewish customs and make them fun for the whole family, this complete sourcebook details activities for holidays at home and travel away from home with clearly illustrated, easy-to-follow instructions.

Naomi Black, *Celebrations: The Book of Jewish Festivals.* Middle Village, N.Y.: Jonathan David, 1989.

This is a lavishly illustrated book that contains information on major Jewish festivals and includes many recipes.

Nina Beth Cardin, *The Tapestry of Jewish Time: A Spiritual Guide to Holidays and Life-Cycle Events.* South Orange, N.J.: Behrman House, 2000.

An illuminating guide that traces the roots of holidays and life-cycle events and suggests how to reclaim and incorporate Jewish rituals and tradition into our lives.

Irving Greenberg, *The Jewish Way: Living the Holidays.* New York: Touchstone Books, 1993.

A thoughtful and comprehensive guide to the Jewish calendar by one of today's foremost Jewish theologians.

Ronald Isaacs and Kerry M. Olitzky, *Sacred Celebrations: A Jewish Holiday Handbook.* Hoboken, N.J.: KTAV Publishing, 1994.

An accessible introductory book for the family celebration of Jewish holidays.

Ron Wolfson, *Hanukkah, 2nd Ed.: The Family Guide to Spiritual Celebration.* Woodstock, Vt.: Jewish Lights Publishing, 2002.

Offers hands-on advice and practical suggestions for every aspect of family celebration.

———, *Passover, 2nd Ed.: The Family Guide to Spiritual Celebration.* Woodstock, Vt.: Jewish Lights Publishing, 2003.

This complete guide presents the concepts, ritual, and ceremony of Passover with step-by-step procedures for observance.

———, *Shabbat, 2nd Ed.: The Family Guide to Preparing For and Celebrating the Sabbath.* Woodstock, Vt.: Jewish Lights Publishing, 2002.

An instructional how-to guide for the beginner and the experienced, it includes information about every aspect of the holy day and all the resources needed to prepare for and celebrate it.

JEWISH HOME LIFE

Joan Nathan, *Jewish Cooking in America.* New York: Knopf, 1998.

———, *The Jewish Holiday Kitchen.* New York: Schocken Books, 1998.

This author is considered the authority on contemporary and classic Jewish cooking and draws on recipes from all over the world. Her books often include background information and kitchen wisdom.

Blu Greenberg, *How to Run a Traditional Jewish Household.* New York: Simon and Schuster, 1985.

A helpful and very comprehensive guide by a leading Orthodox Jewish feminist thinker.

Notes

Notes

About JEWISH LIGHTS Publishing

People of all faiths and backgrounds yearn for books that attract, engage, educate, and spiritually inspire.

Our principal goal is to stimulate thought and help all people learn about who the Jewish People are, where they come from, and what the future can be made to hold. While people of our diverse Jewish heritage are the primary audience, our books speak to people in the Christian world as well and will broaden their understanding of Judaism and the roots of their own faith.

We bring to you authors who are at the forefront of spiritual thought and experience. While each has something different to say, they all say it in a voice that you can hear.

Our books are designed to welcome you and then to engage, stimulate, and inspire. We judge our success not only by whether or not our books are beautiful and commercially successful, but by whether or not they make a difference in your life.

We at Jewish Lights take great care to produce beautiful books that present meaningful spiritual content in a form that reflects the art of making high quality books. Therefore, we want to acknowledge those who contributed to the production of this book.

Stuart M. Matlins

Stuart M. Matlins, Publisher

PRODUCTION
Sara Dismukes, Tim Holtz,
Martha McKinney & Bridgett Taylor

EDITORIAL
Rebecca Castellano, Amanda Dupuis, Polly Short Mahoney,
Lauren Seidman & Emily Wichland

TYPESETTING
Kristin Goble, PerfecType, Nashville, Tennessee

COVER DESIGN
Bridgett Taylor

COVER / TEXT PRINTING & BINDING
Lake Book, Melrose Park, Illinois

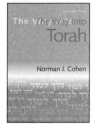   

Spirituality/Jewish Meditation

Aleph-Bet Yoga
Embodying the Hebrew Letters for Physical and Spiritual Well-Being
by *Steven A. Rapp;* Foreword by *Tamar Frankiel & Judy Greenfeld;* Preface by *Hart Lazer*

Blends aspects of hatha yoga and the shapes of the Hebrew letters. Connects yoga practice with Jewish spiritual life. Easy-to-follow instructions, b/w photos.

7 x 10, 128 pp, Quality PB, b/w photos, ISBN 1-58023-162-4 **$16.95**

The Rituals & Practices of a Jewish Life
A Handbook for Personal Spiritual Renewal
by *Rabbi Kerry M. Olitzky* and *Rabbi Daniel Judson;* Foreword by *Vanessa L. Ochs;* Illustrated by *Joel Moskowitz*

This easy-to-use handbook explains the why, what, and how of ten specific areas of Jewish ritual and practice: morning and evening blessings, covering the head, blessings throughout the day, daily prayer, tefillin, tallit and *tallit katan*, Torah study, kashrut, *mikvah*, and entering Shabbat.

6 x 9, 272 pp, Quality PB, Illus., ISBN 1-58023-169-1 **$18.95**

Discovering Jewish Meditation: *Instruction & Guidance for Learning an Ancient Spiritual Practice* by Nan Fink Gefen 6 x 9, 208 pp, Quality PB, ISBN 1-58023-067-9 **$16.95**

The Handbook of Jewish Meditation Practices: *A Guide for Enriching the Sabbath and Other Days of Your Life* by Rabbi David A. Cooper
6 x 9, 208 pp, Quality PB, ISBN 1-58023-102-0 **$16.95**

Meditation from the Heart of Judaism: *Today's Teachers Share Their Practices, Techniques, and Faith* Ed. by Avram Davis 6 x 9, 256 pp, Quality PB, ISBN 1-58023-049-0 **$16.95**

The Way of Flame: *A Guide to the Forgotten Mystical Tradition of Jewish Meditation* by Avram Davis 4½ x 8, 176 pp, Quality PB, ISBN 1-58023-060-1 **$15.95**

Minding the Temple of the Soul: *Balancing Body, Mind, and Spirit through Traditional Jewish Prayer, Movement, and Meditation* by Tamar Frankiel and Judy Greenfeld
7 x 10, 184 pp, Quality PB, Illus., ISBN 1-879045-64-8 **$16.95**

Entering the Temple of Dreams: *Jewish Prayers, Movements, and Meditations for the End of the Day* by Tamar Frankiel and Judy Greenfeld
7 x 10, 192 pp, Illus., Quality PB, ISBN 1-58023-079-2 **$16.95**

Spirituality

My People's Prayer Book: *Traditional Prayers, Modern Commentaries*
Ed. by *Dr. Lawrence A. Hoffman*

Provides a diverse and exciting commentary to the traditional liturgy, helping modern men and women find new wisdom in Jewish prayer, and bring liturgy into their lives. Each book includes Hebrew text, modern translation, and commentaries *from all perspectives* of the Jewish world.
Vol. 1—*The Sh'ma and Its Blessings*, 7 x 10, 168 pp, HC, ISBN 1-879045-79-6 **$23.95**
Vol. 2—*The Amidah*, 7 x 10, 240 pp, HC, ISBN 1-879045-80-X **$23.95**
Vol. 3—*P'sukei D'zimrah* (Morning Psalms), 7 x 10, 240 pp, HC, ISBN 1-879045-81-8 **$24.95**
Vol. 4—*Seder K'riat Hatorah* (The Torah Service), 7 x 10, 264 pp, HC, ISBN 1-879045-82-6 **$23.95**
Vol. 5—*Birkhot Hashachar* (Morning Blessings), 7 x 10, 240 pp, HC, ISBN 1-879045-83-4 **$24.95**
Vol. 6—*Tachanun and Concluding Prayers*, 7 x 10, 240 pp, HC, ISBN 1-879045-84-2 **$24.95**

Six Jewish Spiritual Paths: *A Rationalist Looks at Spirituality*
by Rabbi Rifat Sonsino
6 x 9, 208 pp, Quality PB, ISBN 1-58023-167-5 **$16.95**; HC, ISBN 1-58023-095-4 **$21.95**

Becoming a Congregation of Learners
Learning as a Key to Revitalizing Congregational Life by Isa Aron, Ph.D.;
Foreword by Rabbi Lawrence A. Hoffman, Co-Developer, Synagogue 2000
6 x 9, 304 pp, Quality PB, ISBN 1-58023-089-X **$19.95**

Self, Struggle & Change
Family Conflict Stories in Genesis and Their Healing Insights for Our Lives
by Dr. Norman J. Cohen 6 x 9, 224 pp, Quality PB, ISBN 1-879045-66-4 **$16.95**

Voices from Genesis: *Guiding Us through the Stages of Life*
by Dr. Norman J. Cohen 6 x 9, 192 pp, Quality PB, ISBN 1-58023-118-7 **$16.95**

Ancient Secrets: *Using the Stories of the Bible to Improve Our Everyday Lives*
by Rabbi Levi Meier, Ph.D. 5½ x 8½, 288 pp, Quality PB, ISBN 1-58023-064-4 **$16.95**

The Business Bible: *10 New Commandments for Bringing Spirituality &*
Ethical Values into the Workplace
by Rabbi Wayne Dosick 5½ x 8½, 208 pp, Quality PB, ISBN 1-58023-101-2 **$14.95**

Being God's Partner: *How to Find the Hidden Link Between Spirituality and Your Work*
by Rabbi Jeffrey K. Salkin; Intro. by Norman Lear AWARD WINNER!
6 x 9, 192 pp, Quality PB, ISBN 1-879045-65-6 **$16.95**; HC, ISBN 1-879045-37-0 **$19.95**

God & the Big Bang
Discovering Harmony Between Science & Spirituality AWARD WINNER!
by Daniel C. Matt 6 x 9, 224 pp, Quality PB, ISBN 1-879045-89-3 **$16.95**

Soul Judaism: *Dancing with God into a New Era*
by Rabbi Wayne Dosick 5½ x 8½, 304 pp, Quality PB, ISBN 1-58023-053-9 **$16.95**

Finding Joy: *A Practical Spiritual Guide to Happiness* AWARD WINNER!
by Rabbi Dannel I. Schwartz with Mark Hass
6 x 9, 192 pp, Quality PB, ISBN 1-58023-009-1 **$14.95**; HC, ISBN 1-879045-53-2 **$19.95**

Children's Spirituality

Cain & Abel   AWARD WINNER!
Finding the Fruits of Peace
by *Sandy Eisenberg Sasso*
Full-color illus. by *Joani Keller Rothenberg*

For ages 5 & up

A sensitive recasting of the ancient tale shows we have the power to deal with anger in positive ways. Provides questions for kids and adults to explore together. "Editor's Choice"—American Library Association's *Booklist*

9 x 12, 32 pp, HC, Full-color illus., ISBN 1-58023-123-3 **$16.95**

For Heaven's Sake   AWARD WINNER!
For ages 4 & up

by *Sandy Eisenberg Sasso*; Full-color illus. by *Kathryn Kunz Finney*
Everyone talked about heaven, but no one would say what heaven was or how to find it. So Isaiah decides to find out. 9 x 12, 32 pp, HC, Full-color illus., ISBN 1-58023-054-7 **$16.95**

God Said Amen   AWARD WINNER!
For ages 4 & up

by *Sandy Eisenberg Sasso*; Full-color illus. by *Avi Katz*
Inspiring tale of two kingdoms: one overflowing with water but without oil to light its lamps; the other blessed with oil but no water to grow its gardens. The kingdoms' rulers ask God for help but are too stubborn to ask each other. Shows that we need only reach out to each other to find God's answer to our prayers. 9 x 12, 32 pp, HC, Full-color illus., ISBN 1-58023-080-6 **$16.95**

God in Between   AWARD WINNER!
For ages 4 & up

by *Sandy Eisenberg Sasso*; Full-color illus. by *Sally Sweetland*
If you wanted to find God, where would you look? This magical, mythical tale teaches that God can be found where we are: within all of us and the relationships between us.
9 x 12, 32 pp, HC, Full-color illus., ISBN 1-879045-86-9 **$16.95**

A Prayer for the Earth: *The Story of Naamah, Noah's Wife*
For ages 4 & up

by *Sandy Eisenberg Sasso*; Full-color illus. by *Bethanne Andersen* AWARD WINNER!
Opens religious imaginations to new ideas about the story of the Flood. When God tells Noah to bring the animals onto the ark, God also calls on Naamah, Noah's wife, to save each plant on Earth. 9 x 12, 32 pp, HC, Full-color illus., ISBN 1-879045-60-5 **$16.95**

But God Remembered   AWARD WINNER!
Stories of Women from Creation to the Promised Land
For ages 8 & up

by *Sandy Eisenberg Sasso*; Full-color illus. by *Bethanne Andersen*
Vibrantly brings to life four stories of courageous and strong women from ancient tradition; all teach important values through their actions and faith.
9 x 12, 32 pp, HC, Full-color illus., ISBN 1-879045-43-5 **$16.95**

Children's Spirituality

In Our Image
God's First Creatures AWARD WINNER!
by *Nancy Sohn Swartz*
Full-color illus. by *Melanie Hall*

For ages 4 & up

A playful new twist on the Creation story—from the perspective of the animals. Celebrates the interconnectedness of nature and the harmony of all living things. "The vibrantly colored illustrations nearly leap off the page in this delightful interpretation." —*School Library Journal*
9 x 12, 32 pp, HC, Full-color illus., ISBN 1-879045-99-0 **$16.95**

God's Paintbrush AWARD WINNER!
For ages 4 & up

by *Sandy Eisenberg Sasso*; Full-color illus. by *Annette Compton*

Invites children of all faiths and backgrounds to encounter God openly in their own lives. Wonderfully interactive; provides questions adult and child can explore together at the end of each episode. 11 x 8½, 32 pp, HC, Full-color illus., ISBN 1-879045-22-2 **$16.95**

Also available: **A Teacher's Guide: A Guide for Jewish & Christian Educators and Parents**
8½ x 11, 32 pp, PB, ISBN 1-879045-57-5 **$8.95**

God's Paintbrush Celebration Kit 9½ x 12, HC, Includes 5 sessions/40 full-color Activity Sheets and Teacher Folder with complete instructions, ISBN 1-58023-050-4 **$21.95**

In God's Name AWARD WINNER!
For ages 4 & up

by *Sandy Eisenberg Sasso*; Full-color illus. by *Phoebe Stone*

Like an ancient myth in its poetic text and vibrant illustrations, this award-winning modern fable about the search for God's name celebrates the diversity and, at the same time, the unity of all people. 9 x 12, 32 pp, HC, Full-color illus., ISBN 1-879045-26-5 **$16.95**

What Is God's Name? (A Board Book)
For ages 0–4

An abridged board book version of award-winning *In God's Name.*
5 x 5, 24 pp, Board, Full-color illus., ISBN 1-893361-10-1 **$7.95** A SKYLIGHT PATHS Book

The 11th Commandment: *Wisdom from Our Children*
For all ages

by *The Children of America* AWARD WINNER!

"If there were an Eleventh Commandment, what would it be?" Children of many religious denominations across America answer this question—in their own drawings and words. "A rare book of spiritual celebration for all people, of all ages, for all time."—*Bookviews*
8 x 10, 48 pp, HC, Full color illus., ISBN 1 879045 46 X **$16.95**

Children's Spirituality

Because Nothing Looks Like God
by *Lawrence and Karen Kushner*
Full-color illus. by *Dawn W. Majewski*

For ages 4 & up

MULTICULTURAL, NONDENOMINATIONAL, NONSECTARIAN

What is God like? The first collaborative work by husband-and-wife team Lawrence and Karen Kushner introduces children to the possibilities of spiritual life. Real-life examples of happiness and sadness—from goodnight stories, to the hope and fear felt the first time at bat, to the closing moments of life—invite us to explore, together with our children, the questions we all have about God, no matter what our age.

11 x 8½, 32 pp, HC, Full-color illus., ISBN 1-58023-092-X **$16.95**

Also available: **Teacher's Guide**, 8½ x 11, 22 pp, PB, ISBN 1-58023-140-3 **$6.95** For ages 5–8

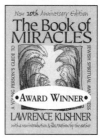

Where Is God?
What Does God Look Like?
How Does God Make Things Happen? (Board Books)

For ages 0–4

by *Lawrence and Karen Kushner*; Full-color illus. by *Dawn W. Majewski*

Gently invites children to become aware of God's presence all around them. Three board books abridged from *Because Nothing Looks Like God* by Lawrence and Karen Kushner.
Each 5 x 5, 24 pp, Board, Full-color illus. **$7.95**   SKYLIGHT PATHS Books

Sharing Blessings
Children's Stories for Exploring the Spirit of the Jewish Holidays

For ages 6 & up

by *Rahel Musleah* and *Rabbi Michael Klayman*; Full-color illus.

What is the spiritual message of each of the Jewish holidays? How do we teach it to our children? Through stories about one family's life, *Sharing Blessings* explores ways to get into the *spirit* of thirteen different holidays.
8½ x 11, 64 pp, HC, Full-color illus., ISBN 1-879045-71-0 **$18.95**

The Book of Miracles   AWARD WINNER!
A Young Person's Guide to Jewish Spiritual Awareness

For ages 9 & up

by *Lawrence Kushner*

Introduces kids to a way of everyday spiritual thinking to last a lifetime. Kushner, whose award-winning books have brought spirituality to life for countless adults, now shows young people how to use Judaism as a foundation on which to build their lives.
6 x 9, 96 pp, HC, 2-color illus., ISBN 1-879045-78-8 **$16.95**

Theology/Philosophy

Love and Terror in the God Encounter
The Theological Legacy of Rabbi Joseph B. Soloveitchik
by *Dr. David Hartman*

Renowned scholar David Hartman explores the sometimes surprising intersection of Soloveitchik's rootedness in halakhic tradition with his genuine responsiveness to modern Western theology. An engaging look at one of the most important Jewish thinkers of the twentieth century.
6 x 9, 240 pp, HC, ISBN 1-58023-112-8 **$25.00**

These Are the Words: *A Vocabulary of Jewish Spiritual Life*
by *Arthur Green*

What are the most essential ideas, concepts and terms that an educated person needs to know about Judaism? From *Adonai* (My Lord) to *zekhut* (merit), this enlightening and entertaining journey through Judaism teaches us the 149 core Hebrew words that constitute the basic vocabulary of Jewish spiritual life. 6 x 9, 304 pp, Quality PB, ISBN 1-58023-107-1 **$18.95**

Broken Tablets: *Restoring the Ten Commandments and Ourselves*
Ed. by *Rabbi Rachel S. Mikva*; Intro. by *Rabbi Lawrence Kushner* AWARD WINNER!

Twelve outstanding spiritual leaders each share profound and personal thoughts about these biblical commands and why they have such a special hold on us.
6 x 9, 192 pp, Quality PB, ISBN 1-58023-158-6 **$16.95**; HC, ISBN 1-58023-066-0 **$21.95**

A Heart of Many Rooms: *Celebrating the Many Voices within Judaism* AWARD WINNER!
by Dr. David Hartman 6 x 9, 352 pp, Quality PB, ISBN 1-58023-156-X **$19.95**;
HC, ISBN 1-58023-048-2 **$24.95**

A Living Covenant: *The Innovative Spirit in Traditional Judaism* AWARD WINNER!
by Dr. David Hartman 6 x 9, 368 pp, Quality PB, ISBN 1-58023-011-3 **$18.95**

Evolving Halakhah: *A Progressive Approach to Traditional Jewish Law*
by Rabbi Dr. Moshe Zemer 6 x 9, 480 pp, HC, ISBN 1-58023-002-4 **$40.00**

The Death of Death: *Resurrection and Immortality in Jewish Thought* AWARD WINNER!
by Dr. Neil Gillman 6 x 9, 336 pp, Quality PB, ISBN 1-58023-081-4 **$18.95**

The Last Trial: *On the Legends and Lore of the Command to Abraham to Offer Isaac as a Sacrifice* by Shalom Spiegel 6 x 9, 208 pp, Quality PB, ISBN 1-879045-29-X **$17.95**

Tormented Master: *The Life and Spiritual Quest of Rabbi Nahman of Bratslav*
by Dr. Arthur Green 6 x 9, 416 pp, Quality PB, ISBN 1-879045-11-7 **$18.95**

The Earth Is the Lord's: *The Inner World of the Jew in Eastern Europe*
by Abraham Joshua Heschel 5½ x 8, 128 pp, Quality PB, ISBN 1-879045-42-7 **$14.95**

A Passion for Truth: *Despair and Hope in Hasidism* by Abraham Joshua Heschel
5½ x 8, 352 pp, Quality PB, ISBN 1-879045-41-9 **$18.95**

Your Word Is Fire: *The Hasidic Masters on Contemplative Prayer* Ed. by Dr. Arthur Green and Dr. Barry W. Holtz 6 x 9, 160 pp, Quality PB, ISBN 1-879045-25-7 **$15.95**

Healing/Wellness/Recovery

Jewish Paths toward Healing and Wholeness
A Personal Guide to Dealing with Suffering
by *Rabbi Kerry M. Olitzky*; Foreword by *Debbie Friedman*

Why me? Why do we suffer? How can we heal? Grounded in personal experience with illness and Jewish spiritual traditions, this book provides healing rituals, psalms and prayers that help readers initiate a dialogue with God, to guide them along the complicated path of healing and wholeness. 6 x 9, 192 pp, Quality PB, ISBN 1-58023-068-7 **$15.95**

Healing of Soul, Healing of Body
Spiritual Leaders Unfold the Strength & Solace in Psalms
Ed. by *Rabbi Simkha Y. Weintraub, CSW*, for The National Center for Jewish Healing

For those who are facing illness and those who care for them. Inspiring commentaries on ten psalms for healing by eminent spiritual leaders reflecting all Jewish movements make the power of the psalms accessible to all.
6 x 9, 128 pp, Quality PB, Illus., 2-color text, ISBN 1-879045-31-1 **$14.95**

Jewish Pastoral Care
A Practical Handbook from Traditional and Contemporary Sources
Ed. by *Rabbi Dayle A. Friedman*

Gives today's Jewish pastoral counselors practical guidelines based in the Jewish tradition.
6 x 9, 464 pp, HC, ISBN 1-58023-078-4 **$35.00**

Twelve Jewish Steps to Recovery: *A Personal Guide to Turning from Alcoholism & Other Addictions . . . Drugs, Food, Gambling, Sex . . .* by Rabbi Kerry M. Olitzky & Stuart A. Copans, M.D. Preface by Abraham J. Twerski, M.D.; "Getting Help" by JACS Foundation 6 x 9, 144 pp, Quality PB, ISBN 1-879045-09-5 **$13.95**

One Hundred Blessings Every Day: *Daily Twelve Step Recovery Affirmations, Exercises for Personal Growth & Renewal Reflecting Seasons of the Jewish Year* by Rabbi Kerry M. Olitzky 4½ x 6½, 432 pp, Quality PB, ISBN 1-879045-30-3 **$14.95**

Recovery from Codependence: *A Jewish Twelve Steps Guide to Healing Your Soul* by Rabbi Kerry M. Olitzky 6 x 9, 160 pp, Quality PB, ISBN 1-879045-32-X **$13.95**

Renewed Each Day: *Daily Twelve Step Recovery Meditations Based on the Bible* by Rabbi Kerry M. Olitzky & Aaron Z. *Vol. I: Genesis & Exodus*; *Vol. II: Leviticus, Numbers and Deuteronomy*
Vol. I: 6 x 9, 224 pp, Quality PB, ISBN 1-879045-12-5 **$14.95**
Vol. II: 6 x 9, 280 pp, Quality PB, ISBN 1-879045-13-3 **$14.95**

Life Cycle/Grief/Divorce

Divorce Is a Mitzvah: *A Practical Guide to Finding Wholeness and Holiness When Your Marriage Dies*
by *Rabbi Perry Netter;*
Afterword—"Afterwards: New Jewish Divorce Rituals"—by *Rabbi Laura Geller*
What does Judaism tell you about divorce? This first-of-its-kind handbook provides practical wisdom from biblical and rabbinic teachings and modern psychological research, as well as information and strength from a Jewish perspective for those experiencing the challenging life-transition of divorce. 6 x 9, 224 pp, Quality PB, ISBN 1-58023-172-1 **$16.95**

Against the Dying of the Light
A Parent's Story of Love, Loss and Hope
by *Leonard Fein*
The sudden death of a child. A personal tragedy beyond description. Rage and despair deeper than sorrow. What can come from it? Raw wisdom and defiant hope. In this unusual exploration of heartbreak and healing, Fein chronicles the sudden death of his 30-year-old daughter and reveals what the progression of grief can teach each one of us.
5½ x 8½, 176 pp, HC, ISBN 1-58023-110-1 **$19.95**

Mourning & Mitzvah, 2nd Ed.: *A Guided Journal for Walking the Mourner's Path through Grief to Healing* with Over 60 Guided Exercises
by *Anne Brener, L.C.S.W.*
For those who mourn a death, for those who would help them, for those who face a loss of any kind, Brener teaches us the power and strength available to us in the fully experienced mourning process. Revised and expanded. 7½ x 9, 304 pp, Quality PB, ISBN 1-58023-113-6 **$19.95**

Grief in Our Seasons: *A Mourner's Kaddish Companion*
by *Rabbi Kerry M. Olitzky*
A wise and inspiring selection of sacred Jewish writings and a simple, powerful ancient ritual for mourners to read each day, to help hold the memory of their loved ones in their hearts. Offers a comforting, step-by-step daily link to saying Kaddish.
4½ x 6½, 448 pp, Quality PB, ISBN 1-879045-55-9 **$15.95**

Tears of Sorrow, Seeds of Hope
A Jewish Spiritual Companion for Infertility and Pregnancy Loss
by Rabbi Nina Beth Cardin 6 x 9, 192 pp, HC, ISBN 1-58023-017-2 **$19.95**

A Time to Mourn, A Time to Comfort
A Guide to Jewish Bereavement and Comfort
by Dr. Ron Wolfson 7 x 9, 336 pp, Quality PB, ISBN 1-879045-96-6 **$18.95**

When a Grandparent Dies
A Kid's Own Remembering Workbook for Dealing with Shiva and the Year Beyond
by Nechama Liss-Levinson, Ph.D.
8 x 10, 48 pp, HC, Illus., 2-color text, ISBN 1-879045-44-3 **$15.95** For ages 7–13

Spirituality—The Kushner Series
Books by Lawrence Kushner

The Way Into Jewish Mystical Tradition

Explains the principles of Jewish mystical thinking, their religious and spiritual significance, and how they relate to our lives. A book that allows us to experience and understand the Jewish mystical approach to our place in the world.
6 x 9, 224 pp, HC, ISBN 1-58023-029-6 **$21.95**

Jewish Spirituality: *A Brief Introduction for Christians*

Addresses Christian's questions, revealing the essence of Judaism in a way that people whose own tradition traces its roots to Judaism can understand and appreciate.
5½ x 8½, 112 pp, Quality PB, ISBN 1-58023-150-0 **$12.95**

Eyes Remade for Wonder: *The Way of Jewish Mysticism and Sacred Living*
A Lawrence Kushner Reader Intro. by *Thomas Moore*

Whether you are new to Kushner or a devoted fan, you'll find inspiration here. With samplings from each of Kushner's works, and a generous amount of new material, this book is to be read and reread, each time discovering deeper layers of meaning in our lives.
6 x 9, 240 pp, Quality PB, ISBN 1-58023-042-3 **$18.95**; HC, ISBN 1-58023-014-8 **$23.95**

Invisible Lines of Connection: *Sacred Stories of the Ordinary* AWARD WINNER!
5½ x 8½, 160 pp, Quality PB, ISBN 1-879045-98-2 **$15.95**

Honey from the Rock: *An Introduction to Jewish Mysticism* SPECIAL ANNIVERSARY EDITION
6 x 9, 176 pp, Quality PB, ISBN 1-58023-073-3 **$15.95**

The Book of Letters: *A Mystical Hebrew Alphabet* AWARD WINNER!
Popular HC Edition, 6 x 9, 80 pp, 2-color text, ISBN 1-879045-00-1 **$24.95**; *Deluxe Gift Edition,* 9 x 12, 80 pp, HC, 4-color text, ornamentation, slipcase, ISBN 1-879045-01-X **$79.95**; *Collector's Limited Edition,* 9 x 12, 80 pp, HC, gold-embossed pages, hand-assembled slipcase. With silkscreened print. Limited to 500 signed and numbered copies, ISBN 1-879045-04-4 **$349.00**

The Book of Words: *Talking Spiritual Life, Living Spiritual Talk* AWARD WINNER!
6 x 9, 160 pp, Quality PB, 2-color text, ISBN 1-58023-020-2 **$16.95**; HC, ISBN 1-879045-35-4 **$21.95**

God Was in This Place & I, i Did Not Know: *Finding Self, Spirituality and Ultimate Meaning*
6 x 9, 192 pp, Quality PB, ISBN 1-879045-33-8 **$16.95**

The River of Light: *Jewish Mystical Awareness* SPECIAL ANNIVERSARY EDITION
6 x 9, 192 pp, Quality PB, ISBN 1-58023-096-2 **$16.95**

Because Nothing Looks Like God
by Lawrence and Karen Kushner; Full-color illus. by Dawn W. Majewski
11 x 8½, 32 pp, HC, Full-color illus., ISBN 1-58023-092-X **$16.95** **For ages 4 & up**

Women's Spirituality

The Women's Torah Commentary: *New Insights from Women Rabbis on the 54 Weekly Torah Portions* Ed. by *Rabbi Elyse Goldstein*

For the first time, women rabbis provide a commentary on the entire Five Books of Moses. More than twenty-five years after the first woman was ordained a rabbi in America, these inspiring teachers bring their rich perspectives to bear on the biblical text. In a week-by-week format; a perfect gift for others, or for yourself. 6 x 9, 496 pp, HC, ISBN 1-58023-076-8 **$34.95**

Moonbeams: *A Hadassah Rosh Hodesh Guide*
Ed. by *Carol Diament, Ph.D.*

This hands-on "idea book" focuses on *Rosh Hodesh,* the festival of the new moon, as a source of spiritual growth for Jewish women. A complete sourcebook that will initiate or rejuvenate women's study groups, it is also perfect for women preparing for *bat mitzvah,* or for anyone interested in learning more about *Rosh Hodesh* observance and what it has to offer. 8½ x 11, 240 pp, Quality PB, ISBN 1-58023-099-7 **$20.00**

Lifecycles In Two Volumes **Award Winners!**
V. 1: *Jewish Women on Life Passages & Personal Milestones*
Ed. and with Intros. by Rabbi Debra Orenstein
V. 2: *Jewish Women on Biblical Themes in Contemporary Life*
Ed. and with Intros. by Rabbi Debra Orenstein and Rabbi Jane Rachel Litman
V. 1: 6 x 9, 480 pp, Quality PB, ISBN 1-58023-018-0 **$19.95**
V. 2: 6 x 9, 464 pp, Quality PB, ISBN 1-58023-019-9 **$19.95**

ReVisions: *Seeing Torah through a Feminist Lens* **Award Winner!**
by Rabbi Elyse Goldstein 5½ x 8½, 224 pp, Quality PB, ISBN 1-58023-117-9 **$16.95**;
208 pp, HC, ISBN 1-58023-047-4 **$19.95**

The Year Mom Got Religion: *One Woman's Midlife Journey into Judaism*
by Lee Meyerhoff Hendler 6 x 9, 208 pp, Quality PB, ISBN 1-58023-070-9 **$15.95**

Ecology

Torah of the Earth: *Exploring 4,000 Years of Ecology in Jewish Thought*
In 2 Volumes Ed. by *Rabbi Arthur Waskow*

An invaluable key to understanding the intersection of ecology and Judaism. Leading scholars provide a guided tour of Jewish ecological thought.
Vol. 1: *Biblical Israel & Rabbinic Judaism,* 6 x 9, 272 pp, Quality PB, ISBN 1-58023-086-5 **$19.95**
Vol. 2: *Zionism & Eco-Judaism,* 6 x 9, 336 pp, Quality PB, ISBN 1-58023-087-3 **$19.95**

Ecology & the Jewish Spirit: *Where Nature & the Sacred Meet* Ed. and with Intros.
by Ellen Bernstein 6 x 9, 288 pp, Quality PB, ISBN 1-58023-082-2 **$16.95**

The Jewish Gardening Cookbook: *Growing Plants & Cooking for Holidays & Festivals*
by Michael Brown 6 x 9, 224 pp, Illus., Quality PB, ISBN 1-58023-116-0 **$16.95**;
HC, ISBN 1-58023-004-0 **$21.95**

Life Cycle & Holidays

The Jewish Family Fun Book: *Holiday Projects, Everyday Activities, and Travel Ideas with Jewish Themes*
by *Danielle Dardashti* & *Roni Sarig*; Illustrated by *Avi Katz*

With almost 100 easy-to-do activities to re-invigorate age-old Jewish customs and make them fun for the whole family, this complete sourcebook details activities for fun at home and away from home, including meaningful everyday and holiday crafts, recipes, travel guides, enriching enter-tainment and much, much more. Illustrated.
6 x 9, 288 pp, Quality PB, Illus., ISBN 1-58023-171-3 **$18.95**

The Book of Jewish Sacred Practices
CLAL's Guide to Everyday & Holiday Rituals & Blessings
Ed. by *Rabbi Irwin Kula* & *Vanessa L. Ochs, Ph.D.*

A meditation, blessing, profound Jewish teaching, and ritual for more than one hundred everyday events and holidays. 6 x 9, 368 pp, Quality PB, ISBN 1-58023-152-7 **$18.95**

Celebrating Your New Jewish Daughter: *Creating Jewish Ways to Welcome Baby Girls into the Covenant—New and Traditional Ceremonies*
by Debra Nussbaum Cohen; Foreword by Rabbi Sandy Eisenberg Sasso
6 x 9, 272 pp, Quality PB, ISBN 1-58023-090-3 **$18.95**

The New Jewish Baby Book AWARD WINNER!
Names, Ceremonies & Customs—A Guide for Today's Families
by Anita Diamant 6 x 9, 336 pp, Quality PB, ISBN 1-879045-28-1 **$18.95**

Parenting As a Spiritual Journey
Deepening Ordinary & Extraordinary Events into Sacred Occasions
by Rabbi Nancy Fuchs-Kreimer 6 x 9, 224 pp, Quality PB, ISBN 1-58023-016-4 **$16.95**

Putting God on the Guest List, 2nd Ed. AWARD WINNER!
How to Reclaim the Spiritual Meaning of Your Child's Bar or Bat Mitzvah
by Rabbi Jeffrey K. Salkin 6 x 9, 224 pp, Quality PB, ISBN 1-879045-59-1 **$16.95**

The Bar/Bat Mitzvah Memory Book: *An Album for Treasuring the Spiritual Celebration* by Rabbi Jeffrey K. Salkin and Nina Salkin
8 x 10, 48 pp, Deluxe HC, 2-color text, ribbon marker, ISBN 1-58023-111-X **$19.95**

For Kids—Putting God on Your Guest List
How to Claim the Spiritual Meaning of Your Bar or Bat Mitzvah
by Rabbi Jeffrey K. Salkin 6 x 9, 144 pp, Quality PB, ISBN 1-58023-015-6 **$14.95**

Bar/Bat Mitzvah Basics, 2nd Ed.: *A Practical Family Guide to Coming of Age Together*
Ed. by Cantor Helen Leneman 6 x 9, 240 pp, Quality PB, ISBN 1-58023-151-9 **$18.95**

Hanukkah, 2nd Ed.: *The Family Guide to Spiritual Celebration*—The Art of Jewish Living
by Dr. Ron Wolfson 7 x 9, 240 pp, Quality PB, Illus., ISBN 1-58023-122-5 **$18.95**

Shabbat, 2nd Ed.: *Preparing for and Celebrating the Sabbath*—The Art of Jewish Living
by Dr. Ron Wolfson 7 x 9, 320 pp, Quality PB, Illus., ISBN 1-58023-164-0 **$19.95**

The Passover Seder—The Art of Jewish Living
by Dr. Ron Wolfson 7 x 9, 352 pp, Quality PB, Illus., ISBN 1-879045-93-1 **$16.95**

Spirituality & More

The Jewish Lights Spirituality Handbook
A Guide to Understanding, Exploring & Living a Spiritual Life
Ed. by *Stuart M. Matlins, Editor in Chief, Jewish Lights Publishing*

Rich, creative material from over fifty spiritual leaders on every aspect of Jewish spirituality today: prayer, meditation, mysticism, study, rituals, special days, the everyday, and more.
6 x 9, 456 pp, Quality PB, ISBN 1-58023-093-8 **$18.95**; HC, ISBN 1-58023-100-4 **$24.95**

The Story of the Jews: *A 4,000-Year Adventure—A Graphic History Book*
Written and illustrated by *Stan Mack*

Through witty cartoons and accurate narrative, illustrates the major characters and events that have shaped the Jewish people and culture. For all ages.
6 x 9, 304 pp, Quality PB, Illus., ISBN 1-58023-155-1 **$16.95**

The Jewish Prophet: *Visionary Words from Moses and Miriam to Henrietta Szold and A. J. Heschel*
by *Rabbi Dr. Michael J. Shire*

This beautifully illustrated collection of Jewish prophecy features the lives and teachings of thirty men and women, from biblical times to modern day. Provides an inspiring and informative description of the role each played in their own time, and an explanation of why we should know about them in our time. Illustrated with illuminations from medieval Hebrew manuscripts.
6½ x 8½, 128 pp, HC, 123 full-color illus., ISBN 1-58023-168-3 **$25.00**

The Enneagram and Kabbalah: *Reading Your Soul*
by Rabbi Howard A. Addison 6 x 9, 176 pp, Quality PB, ISBN 1-58023-001-6 **$15.95**

Cast in God's Image: *Discover Your Personality Type Using the Enneagram and Kabbalah*
by Rabbi Howard A. Addison 7 x 9, 176 pp, Quality PB, ISBN 1-58023-124-1 **$16.95**

Mystery Midrash: *An Anthology of Jewish Mystery & Detective Fiction* AWARD WINNER!
Ed. by Lawrence W. Raphael 6 x 9, 304 pp, Quality PB, ISBN 1-58023-055-5 **$16.95**

Criminal Kabbalah: *An Intriguing Anthology of Jewish Mystery & Detective Fiction*
Ed. by Lawrence W. Raphael; Foreword by Laurie R. King
6 x 9, 256 pp, Quality PB, ISBN 1-58023-109-8 **$16.95**

Sacred Intentions: *Daily Inspiration to Strengthen the Spirit, Based on Jewish Wisdom*
by Rabbi Kerry M. Olitzky & Rabbi Lori Forman
4½ x 6½, 448 pp, Quality PB, ISBN 1-58023-061-X **$15.95**

Restful Reflections: *Nighttime Inspiration to Calm the Soul, Based on Jewish Wisdom*
by Rabbi Kerry M. Olitzky & Rabbi Lori Forman
4½ x 6½, 448 pp, Quality PB, ISBN 1-58023-091-1 **$15.95**

Embracing the Covenant: *Converts to Judaism Talk About Why & How* Ed. by Rabbi Allan Berkowitz & Patti Moskovitz 6 x 9, 192 pp, Quality PB, ISBN 1-879045-50-8 **$16.95**

Wandering Stars: *An Anthology of Jewish Fantasy & Science Fiction* Ed. by Jack Dann; Intro. by Isaac Asimov 6 x 9, 272 pp, Quality PB, ISBN 1-58023-005-9 **$16.95**

Israel—A Spiritual Travel Guide: *A Companion for the Modern Jewish Pilgrim* AWARD WINNER!
by Rabbi Lawrence A. Hoffman 4¾ x 10, 256 pp, Quality PB, ISBN 1-879045-56-7 **$18.95**

Spirituality

The Dance of the Dolphin
Finding Prayer, Perspective and Meaning in the Stories of Our Lives
by *Karyn D. Kedar*

Helps you decode the three "languages" we all must learn—prayer, perspective, meaning—to weave the seemingly ordinary and extraordinary together.
6 x 9, 176 pp, HC, ISBN 1-58023-154-3 **$19.95**

Does the Soul Survive?
A Jewish Journey to Belief in Afterlife, Past Lives & Living with Purpose
by *Rabbi Elie Kaplan Spitz*; Foreword by *Brian L. Weiss, M.D.*

Spitz relates his own experiences and those shared with him by people he has worked with as a rabbi, and shows us that belief in afterlife and past lives, so often approached with reluctance, is in fact true to Jewish tradition.
6 x 9, 288 pp, Quality PB, ISBN 1-58023-165-9 **$16.95**; HC, ISBN 1-58023-094-6 **$21.95**

The Gift of Kabbalah
Discovering the Secrets of Heaven, Renewing Your Life on Earth
by *Tamar Frankiel, Ph.D.*

Makes accessible the mysteries of Kabbalah. Traces Kabbalah's evolution in Judaism and shows us its most important gift: a way of revealing the connection between our "everyday" life and the spiritual oneness of the universe. 6 x 9, 256 pp, HC, ISBN 1-58023-108-X **$21.95**

God Whispers: *Stories of the Soul, Lessons of the Heart*
by Karyn D. Kedar 6 x 9, 176 pp, Quality PB, ISBN 1-58023-088-1 **$15.95**

Bringing the Psalms to Life: *How to Understand and Use the Book of Psalms*
by Rabbi Daniel F. Polish
6 x 9, 208 pp, Quality PB, ISBN 1-58023-157-8 **$16.95**; HC, ISBN 1-58023-077-6 **$21.95**

The Empty Chair: *Finding Hope and Joy—*
Timeless Wisdom from a Hasidic Master, Rebbe Nachman of Breslov **AWARD WINNER!**
4 x 6, 128 pp, Deluxe PB, 2-color text, ISBN 1-879045-67-2 **$9.95**

The Gentle Weapon: *Prayers for Everyday and Not-So-Everyday Moments*
Adapted from the Wisdom of Rebbe Nachman of Breslov
4 x 6, 144 pp, Deluxe PB, 2-color text, ISBN 1-58023-022-9 **$9.95**

Or phone, fax, mail or e-mail to: **JEWISH LIGHTS Publishing**
Sunset Farm Offices, Route 4 • P.O. Box 237 • Woodstock, Vermont 05091
Tel: (802) 457-4000 • Fax: (802) 457-4004 • www.jewishlights.com
Credit card orders: (800) 962-4544 (8:30AM–5:30PM ET Monday–Friday)
Generous discounts on quantity orders. SATISFACTION GUARANTEED. Prices subject to change.